Donna Janke

111 Places
in Winnipeg
That You
Must Not Miss

Photographs by Gindalee Ouskun

emons:

To Rick, Rhea, Taylor, Forest, and Norah
Donna Janke

To Bennett, Drew, and Riven (woof)
Gindalee Ouskun

Bibliographical information of the Deutsche Nationalbibliothek
The Deutsche Nationalbibliothek lists this publication in
the Deutsche Nationalbibliografie; detailed bibliographical data
are available on the internet at http://dnb.d-nb.de.

© Emons Verlag GmbH
All rights reserved
© Photographs by Gindalee Ouskun, except see p. 238
© Cover icon: AdobeStock/justas; Shutterstock/Leigh Prather
Layout: Eva Kraskes, based on a design
by Lübbeke | Naumann | Thoben
Maps: altancicek.design, www.altancicek.de
Basic cartographical information from Openstreetmap,
© OpenStreetMap-Mitwirkende, OdbL
Edited by: Karen E. Seiger
Printing and binding: Grafisches Centrum Cuno, Calbe
Printed in Germany 2024
ISBN 978-3-7408-2080-0
First edition

Guidebooks for Locals & Experienced Travelers
Join us in uncovering new places around the world at
www.111places.com

Foreword

After I discovered the 111 Places series, I kept thinking of places in the city that has been my home for decades. While Winnipeg now gains recognition for all it offers, it was underrated and the butt of jokes for many years. Winnipeggers joked too, but we also knew there was much to love.

Winnipeg sits on land that was a First Nations meeting place for thousands of years, a fur trading centre, and gateway to Canada's developing West. Amidst its award-winning architecture, you'll find heritage buildings and energy-efficient office towers. Old and new combine in a contemporary campus building with a façade of century-old storefronts and a restaurant in a historic pumphouse. A provincial park highlights late-1800s Franco-Manitoban life.

Winnipeggers savour hot summers and embrace the winters that gave the city its nickname Winterpeg. Walk the world's largest snow maze or climb an ice tower. Enjoy all seasons in Canada's largest urban forest. See wood spirits carved into a riverbank forest.

In this culturally diverse city, you can eat modern dishes rooted in traditional First Nations and Métis foods or take a world culinary tour at an ethnic grocery store. Go look for Arctic wildlife art in a back alley. Visit Canada's only museum of craft, and attend Canada's longest-running blues jam session. I was continually reminded of Winnipeg's creative, artistic, and resilient spirit as I worked on this book.

Winnipeg is an unpretentious city with the heart of a small town. The word "community" popped up time and time again during the interviews with the people I wrote about. It's at the core of many places, be it North America's largest non-profit fabrication lab, a co-op hardware store, a centre offering free art programming, or kindness rock gardens.

Have fun discovering the unique character of The Peg. Note that after Winnipeg's bus system changes mid-2025 you'll need to check what new route gets you to your stop.

111 Places

1 _ A Man Called Intrepid
Mural about a real-life spy

Sir William Stephenson (1897–1989) is sometimes considered the inspiration for Ian Fleming's James Bond. Winnipeg-born and raised, Stephenson was a World War I Ace fighter pilot who later became a millionaire entrepreneur. He played an important role in World War II intelligence activities, received over 20 awards and medals, and was knighted in 1945. On the side of the Royal Canadian Legion's former first branch, you'll find a mural in which artist David Carty has incorporated many aspects of the life of the man code-named "Intrepid."

In *A Man Called Intrepid*, is a portrait of Stephenson, several aircraft, a patent document, and the wireless photo transmission device he and a friend developed, a precursor to television. An Enigma machine and Bletchley Park speak to his alerting the British Secret Service (BSS) about the 1930s buildup of German armaments and cipher machines, information gained due to his industrial connections. Letters wafting through air refer to transmitted code. You'll see the words "Shepperton Studios," the famous British film and sound stage in which he invested. A tank represents the film industry's creation of bogus airfields and Army camps to deceive the Germans. Look for the Rockefeller Centre, where Stephenson ran BSS intelligence operations. There's a reference to the spy training camp he created near Oshawa, Ontario. Badges include that of the CIA, which he helped create. Sir Winston Churchill and Commander Ian Fleming figure in the mural, as well as a drawing of Sean Connery, the first movie James Bond.

Was Stephenson really the basis for Bond? In a foreword to *Room 3603*, Fleming (1908–1964) says Bond is a meld of qualities he noted among Secret Service men and a highly romanticized version of a spy. He also says Stephenson was "one of the great secret agents" and "it would be a foolish person who would argue his credentials."

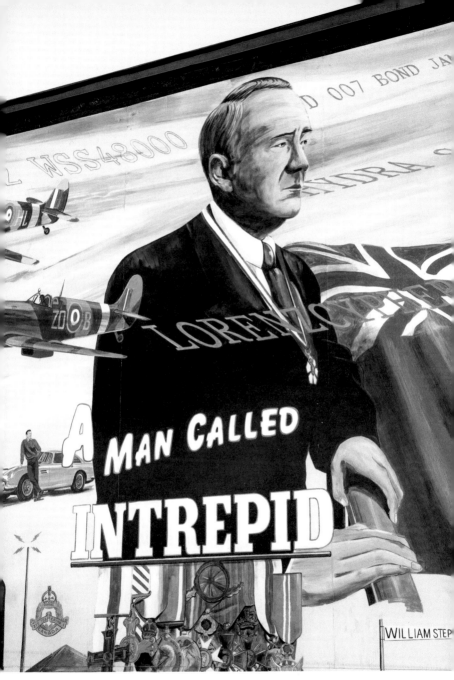

Address 626 Sargent Avenue, Winnipeg, MB R3E 0A3 | Getting there Bus 15 to
Sargent & Maryland (Stops 10402/10482) | Hours Unrestricted | Tip Cross Sargent
Avenue to see *Zoohky*, another popular West End mural that features a local hero, poet, and
artist who spent his days cycling through the area and fixing things (635 Sargent Avenue).

2__Agowiidiwinan Centre

Interactive treaty education display

Many Winnipeg events begin by acknowledging the event is occurring on Treaty 1 territory and acknowledging the land as the ancestral territory of First Nations and the homeland of the Métis nation. Treaty 1 was the first of 11 numbered treaties negotiated between the Crown and First Nations between 1871 and 1921 to facilitate sharing of the land. The treaties remain binding, reciprocal commitments in place today, but many Canadians still know little about them. The Agowiidiwinan Centre, developed by the Treaty Relations Commission of Manitoba, offers a chance to learn more.

Walls of windows and colourful information panels create an inviting space. Laid out in a meandering pattern along a blue path like a river, the panels provide information through eye-catching pictures and readable text. To go deeper, scan the QR codes on the panels with your phone to link to articles, videos, and maps. On display are artifacts such as a ceremonial pipe, a replica of Treaty 5 Chief's jacket, and framed written pages from Treaty 1.

Panels tell of the long history of First Nations treaty-making, with its protocols and ceremonies. You'll find information about pre-Confederation agreements and partnerships. You'll read about the spirit and intent of the numbered treaties. The First Nations viewed the treaties as a way to share the land. The Crown considered the treaties a surrender of the land in exchange for certain rights. Examples of how the treaty principles were not adhered to include the Indian Act, which regulated all aspects of First Nations life, and the pass system, which restricted First Nations' mobility.

All areas of Manitoba are covered by treaty – look for the Manitoba map that shows treaty numbers by area. A better understanding of the treaties is key to sharing responsibility for maintaining the Treaty Relationship because, as a panel states, "We are all Treaty People."

Address 15 Forks Market Road, Winnipeg, MB, +1 (204) 956-1107, www.trcm.ca, administration@trcm.ca | **Getting there** Bus 38 to Forks Market (Stop 10907) | **Hours** Mon–Fri 9am–5pm | **Tip** Treaty No. 1 Legacy Flag Installation at Lower Fort Garry, site of the signing of the treaty, features seven First Nations flags, Canada's flag, and the Union Jack (5925 Highway 9, St. Andrews, https://parks.canada.ca).

3 __ Art City

Community art programming accessible to all

There may not be another art centre like Art City in Canada or anywhere else. The non-profit community art studio offers free art programming to people of all ages on a drop-in basis, and all the materials are free too. A main work space inside its building is lined with supply cabinets, and there is also a digital art room, a dark room, and a ceramics room. During themed workshops in a variety of mediums, facilitators guide participants while still giving them freedom to follow their own artistic paths. You can work on individual creations or collaborate on pieces for public display.

Wanda Koop, internationally renowned artist and community activist, created Art City in the 1990s. Seeing the effect of poverty on the kids in her West Broadway neighbourhood, she started outdoor pop-up art activities. She and area youth collaborated on murals they placed over boarded-up windows. During a chance encounter at a university panel, a philanthropist asked her about her vision. Her dream was opening a storefront property where people make art for free. A pilot program ran in a boarded-up nightclub during the summer of 1998. Today, Art City continues to connect contemporary artists and community members to explore the creative process.

Staff and dedicated volunteers deliver programming developed via community consultation, and one-week residency programs bring artists from various places to share their processes. Art City offers a free hearty and healthy meal program for anyone who is hungry, as well as youth mentorship opportunities. People of all ages are welcome, and the majority of participants are between 6 and 16.

Art City is about making art accessible to everyone, but it is also about more than art. It's about problem-solving, connection, collaboration, transcending barriers, and community. Art becomes a means to envision the world one would like to see.

Address 616 Broadway Avenue, Winnipeg, MB R3C 0W8, +1 (204) 775-9856, www.artcityinc.com, info@artcityinc.com | Getting there Bus 10, 17, 20, or 23 to Broadway & Young (Stops 10207/10208) | Hours See website for seasonal hours | Tip ArtsJunktion (594 Main Street, www.artsjunktion.mb.ca) offers reclaimed arts and crafts supplies on a take-what-you-need, pay-what-you-can basis, runs a tool-lending library, and offers workshops.

4 Assiniboine Forest
Wilderness within the city

The 292-hectare (722-acre) Assiniboine Forest is one of the largest natural urban forests in Canada. Amid oak and aspen trees, you'll find birds, animals, small areas of tall-grass prairie restoration, a constructed wetland area, a wide variety of plants, and a resident herd of white-tail deer. Trails through the forest allow you to leave the city behind without actually leaving it.

The accessible, paved all-season Sagimay Trail is a 1.5-kilometre (0.6-mile) loop. Shortly after entering the forest from the parking lot, you'll pass through a clearing before being surrounded by forest again. The hum of traffic recedes a bit and is replaced by the rustling of the breeze through the trees and the singing of birds. You'll come to Eve Werier Pond, dedicated to environmentalist and preservationist Eve Werier. An observation deck overlooking the pond is a good spot from which to watch waterfowl. You can walk a wood-chip path around the pond. There is a short boardwalk trail. Other trails, covered with limestone or wood chips, radiate from Sagimay Trail.

It is unusual to find a forest within city limits. This one might not exist had it not been for the stock market crash of 1929. In 1920, the area, then part of the town of Tuxedo, was slated for development. Plans halted with the stock market crash and the subsequent depression. Over the following decades, people used the area for recreation. A few spots became landfill sites. In the 1960s, citizens lobbied to preserve the forest. In 1973, Assiniboine Forest, by then part of Winnipeg, became a municipal nature park. Road cuts created in preparation for development are now trails through the forest. The Charleswood Rotary Club, working with City of Winnipeg naturalists, acts as steward of the forest.

Assiniboine Forest offers a wilderness within the city and a chance for urban dwellers to get close to nature.

Address Corner of Grant Avenue and Chalfont Road, Winnipeg, MB R3R 3V4, www.winnipeg.ca | Getting there Bus 66 to Grant & Chalfont (Stops 60525/60526) | Hours Unrestricted | Tip Situated along a former railway line, the 6.5-kilometre Harte Trail, part of which runs through the south end of Assiniboine Forest, is great for hiking or cycling (www.hartetrail.com).

5 Aurora Farm

Earth-friendly, animal-loving, solar-powered farm

On small group tours at Aurora Farm, you'll interact up close with the animals, hear about Indigenous planting practices, and discover the farm's commitment to sustainability. As you pet heritage chickens, goats, alpacas, and horses, you'll learn their names and personalities. The farm's most well-known product is goat milk soap. Alpaca fleece is sold as raw fleece, yarn, or knitted products. Sustainable practices include rain water collection and large-scale composting. Solar panels generate power for the farm. The farm sells its natural products, including produce, herbs, and edible flowers, in its on-site store as well as to consumers and wholesalers through Firewood Food Hub. The store also stocks items from other Manitoba artisans.

Louise May, who has a degree in Environmental Studies, purchased the farm in 2004 to be closer to nature, raise her own food, and give her children an environmentally friendly lifestyle. She did not set out to create a business. The farm evolved over the years as she studied permaculture design, composting, organic gardening, eco-diversity, and animal management. She became involved with Worldwide Opportunities on Organic Farms, Canada (WWOOF Canada), part of a worldwide effort that matches organic farms with people who want organic farm experiences. She started making goat soap and selling it at the St. Norbert Farmers' Market. She is an avid knitter and crocheter who has always loved alpacas. She acquired three Indigenous pony mares when she became part of a caretaker society working to bring them out of near extinction. The small but robust breed of forest ponies existed in North America prior to European contact, but only 200 or so remain in the world today.

Experience what the farm has to offer by taking the tour or by attending one of Aurora Farm's events, such as goat and alpaca yoga classes or soap-making workshops.

Address 4265 Waverley Street, Winnipeg, MB R3V 1W8, +1 (204) 261-6279, www.aurorafarm.ca, info@aurorafarm.ca | Getting there By car, take Perimeter Highway, go south on Waverley Street | Hours Fri–Sun 11am–4pm | Tip Tours at Winnipeg's Little Red Barn Sanctuary, home to rescued farm animals, allow participants to interact with the animals while learning empathy and compassion. Book tours online, and location details will be shared at that time (www.thelittleredbarn.org).

6 _ Back Alley Arctic
Arctic wildlife art gallery in a back lane

A walk through a back lane is rarely something you'd recommend to others, but there is one such lane in the eclectic, artistic neighbourhood of Wolseley, known as Winnipeg's "Granola Belt," that you won't want to miss. Garage doors, fences, and back yards feature stunning paintings of Arctic wildlife by artist and activist Kal Barteski. But she didn't set out to create an outdoor art gallery.

It started in 2017, when Barteski painted a large polar bear head on her garage door as a way to practice creating murals on metal. Upon seeing the image, a neighbour asked if she'd paint one on his garage door. Other neighbours expressed interest. Barteski, who is passionate about Arctic animals and an advocate for the wild, offered to paint Arctic wildlife images for free on the garage doors of anyone along the lane who wanted one. For neighbours who were interested but didn't have a garage, she painted animals on sheets of corrugated plastic to be placed in yards or attached to fences. You'll now find polar bears, beluga whales, foxes, a wolf, caribou, walrus, and other wildlife decorating both sides of the lane. Many paintings contain the ink drips Barteski leaves to celebrate imperfection.

Not only do the paintings beautify the neighbourhood, but they foster a greater sense of community. Neighbours hold potlucks in the lane and know each other by the animals painted on their properties. Now known as *Back Alley Arctic*, the collection attracts both locals and tourists. Families stroll through the lane. Teachers from two nearby schools bring their students and talk about the animals. The Winnipeg Trolley Company city bus tour makes a stop here too. Barteski says it shows how transformative public art can be and the resilience of what can be done with a little bit of effort and paint. She hopes you experience a magical moment in the middle of a busy city.

Address Back alley of Canora & Ethelbert Streets between Westminster & Wolseley Avenues, Winnipeg, MB, www.kalbarteski.com | **Getting there** Bus 10 to Wolseley & Canora (Stop 11057) or Wolseley & Palmerston (Stop 11054) | **Hours** Unrestricted | **Tip** The aptly named Next Door, a restaurant led by the female-run Good Neighbour Brewery Inc. located beside it, is a lively gathering space (116 Sherbrook Street, www.goodneighbourbrewing.com).

7 — Baked Expectations
Manitoba's famous Shmoo Torte

Inspired by bar mitzvah dessert tables and a tradition of Jewish women in Winnipeg baking for lifecycle events, Beth Grubert opened Baked Expectations in 1983. The former Glow's Pharmacy, an Osborne Village building with a distinctive curved glass front wall, became the dessert restaurant's home, and Shmoo Torte was on the menu.

Made with layers of pecan-flavoured angel food cake filled with whipped cream and served with a buttery caramel sauce, Shmoo Torte (also Schmoo Torte) has been a Manitoba favourite ever since a Winnipeg mother created it for her son's bar mitzvah in 1948. Dora Zaslavsky, a Russian immigrant with a talent for cooking, began selling delicate dainties to help support her family after her husband became ill. She then catered some weddings and developed a reputation in the Jewish community for her delicious cooking. She opened a catering business that eventually expanded across Canada and the United States. She created Shmoo Torte for the bar mitzvah of her son Murray, who wanted a special cake that wouldn't be found at everyone else's bar mitzvah. It soon became a Winnipeg bar mitzvah standard.

The origin of the torte's name is not clear. It may have been named after shmoos, the fictional cartoon characters in Al Capp's *Li'l Abner* strip. Capp said shmoos, who produced eggs, milk, and butter, were delicious to eat and eager to be eaten. Whether this is the source of the name or not, it seems a good metaphor for the rich cake.

Baked Expectation's original menu featured 10 dessert items. Today, the menu rotates through a larger selection that includes 40 tortes. At any one time, you'll find 12 cheesecakes and 14 tortes, and cherry cheesecake and Shmoo Torte are always on offer. You can order a cake or slices to take home or enjoy slices in the restaurant. Order up hot and cold drinks, wine, craft beer, and liqueur.

Address 161 Osborne Street, Winnipeg, MB R3L 1Y7, +1 (204) 452-5176, www.bakedexpectations.ca | Getting there Bus 16, 18, or 60 to Osborne & Wardlaw (Stop 10185) or Osborne & Stradbrook (Stop 10186) | Hours Open daily, call for hours | Tip The Happy Cooker contains a selection of cookware, bakeware, and kitchen utensils should you wish to try baking your own tortes (464 Stradbrook Avenue, www.thehappycooker.ca).

8_ The Basement

A night out in another era

A Howard Johnson basement may be an unlikely entertainment destination, but The Basement Speakeasy and Comedy Lounge in its Winnipeg West location is a stand-up venue you'll want to visit and revisit.

The Basement, which opened in early 2020, recreates the vibe from another era. Furnishings include vintage sofas and arm chairs, assorted tables and chairs, a curved bar, and red velvet curtains behind the stage. The space, which was once a country bar, had been used as storage for years. When new hotel owners cleaned it out, they retained the wood paneling on the upper walls and the geometric carpet, but they painted the lower walls and ceiling black. The large room now has an intimate, lounge feel.

Come to a live comedy show here on Friday and Saturday nights. Performers include local comedians, as well as comedians from other parts of the continent. Burlesque shows are another audience favourite. Among the drink offerings, you'll find a large selection of custom-created, Prohibition-era-style cocktails. The food menu features appetizers and pub-style food, house-made using local ingredients.

Show ticket seating options include a two-person or four-person VIP sofa; general seating at a selection of regular or bar-height tables; and bar seating, which is the most affordable option. A large table in one corner known as the Boardroom accommodates large groups.

The Basement remains open after each show, so you can linger and soak up the atmosphere or play a game of pool or darts. People who didn't have tickets to the show are welcome to walk in after the show ends and enjoy all The Basement has to offer.

In keeping with the secrecy once associated with speakeasies, the ground level entrance to The Basement is disguised. You enter a small vestibule that appears to be a janitor's closet. A door at the back opens up to a staircase that takes you down to the venue.

Address 3740 Portage Avenue, Winnipeg, MB R3K 0Z9, www.basementwpg.com | Getting there Bus 11, 21, 24, or 66 to Portage & Buchanan (Stops 20246/20249) | Hours See website for show times | Tip In the Prohibition-themed escape room at Enigma Escapes, you must identify a crime kingpin in an infamous speakeasy before a bomb goes off (4–980 Lorimer Boulevard, www.enigmaescapes.com).

9 Beaumont Station

A giant kettle symbolizes a lost community

A number of stations along the BLUE Rapid Transit Line host public artworks. The pieces in the Winnipeg Art Council's project *Connecting Roots Along the Red River* speak to the history and stories of the Fort Garry neighbourhood through which the line runs. At Beaumont Station, you'll find the giant *Rooster Town Kettle and Fetching Water*.

Rooster Town, also known as Pakan Town, was a largely Métis community that existed on the outskirts of Winnipeg from 1901 to 1961. The unofficial community had no running water, sewer, electricity, or roads. It was torn down, and its residents were evicted to make way for a mall, a school, and an expanding city neighbourhood. Media stories about the town generally had a racist slant that contributed to public support for the removal of the "shantytown."

Artist Ian August chose an oversized, copper-coloured tea kettle to represent the community. A kettle had a permanent spot on everyone's wood stove, ready to make tea for family and visitors. At its peak, Rooster Town housed 59 families and 250 people, and August's *Rooster Town Kettle* is large enough to boil the minimum amount of daily water needed to sustain a population of 250. August worked with Parr Metal Fabricators to create the stainless-steel structure, which needed to be moved to the site in two pieces.

Rooster Town residents carried or pulled cans of water by sled from a town pump over a kilometre (0.6 miles) away or paid for water to be delivered. Three *Fetching Water* silhouettes placed along a kilometre of the active pathway represent that daily activity and remind us that lack of access to clean water remains a crucial issue in many Indigenous communities.

This work of art reminds us that Rooster Town existed, and they represent the generosity and sharing found in Métis culture. Panels at the site have information about Rooster Town and the sculpture.

Address Georgina Street at Parker Avenue, Winnipeg, MB, +1 (204) 943-7668, www.winnipegarts.ca/public-art/gallery/rooster-town-kettle, info@winnipegarts.ca | Getting there Bus BLUE, 29, 641, or 677 to Beaumont | Hours Unrestricted | Tip The Bill and Helen Norrie Library, beside Rooster Town Park, features a pitched roof, earth tones, and Rooster Town images in recognition of the site's history (15 Poseidon Bay, wpl.winnipeg.ca/library).

10 Bergen Cutoff Bridge

An abandoned rail bridge still stands

As you drive over the Chief Peguis Trail Bridge, you may glimpse an old, steel rail bridge to the South that appears to be standing unconnected to anything in the middle of the Red River. It does indeed stand alone and has remained unused since 1928. According to information from the Manitoba Historical Society, the Bergen Cutoff Bridge was built in 1913 by the Canadian Pacific Railway (CPR) as an alternate route to the company's North Transcona Rail Yards. The Yards were being built at the time to ease pressure on the company's existing yards.

The first train crossing occurred in May 1914 when the Yards opened, but the anticipated rail growth that led to the creation of the Yards didn't materialize. After CPR closed in 1928, the company no longer used the bridge.

The tracks that once connected the bridge with either side of the river have long since been removed. With no remaining land access, the abandoned bridge appears forgotten and forsaken. Not only is this bridge disconnected from land, but it appears to be disconnected from itself. The rotating central section once swung open to allow ships to pass, and it now sits permanently in the "open" position.

On the west side of the river, the bridge is barely visible through the trees from a trail running through Kildonan Park and behind Kildonan Golf Course. In the summer, foliage obscures much of it. The area on the east side of the river is filled with residential development, but the City maintains a tree-lined pathway that runs from the river to Henderson Highway. You can get a better view of the bridge from the river-end of that pathway. Graffiti covers the nearest of the concrete piers supporting the bridge.

Over the years, alternate uses, including a pedestrian pathway or lookout, have been proposed, but nothing has come to fruition. The bridge stands alone, desolate, and uncrossable.

Address Red River near Bergen Cutoff Park, 1235 Kildonan Drive, Winnipeg, MB | Getting there Bus 11 or 77 to Henderson & Slater (Stops 40391/40417) | Hours Daily 7am–10pm | Tip The authentic French restaurant Resto Gare Bistro and Train Bar is housed in a 1913 former train station with a lounge in an attached railcar (630 Des Meurons Street, www.restogare.com).

11   Bison Safari
North America's largest land mammal up close

With winding forest trails, a lake, and interpretative attractions, FortWhyte Alive offers year-round opportunities to connect with nature. Hike or canoe in summer, and snowshoe, skate, toboggan, or ice fish in winter. Look for deer, waterfowl, other wildlife – and bison. That's right. FortWhyte Alive keeps a herd of North America's largest mammals. The "wild" herd lives in large fenced grass fields, where they generally fend for themselves, with a little bit of help from centre staff.

Get a look into the bison enclosure from the viewing station on the North Trail. And for a more up-close experience, take the hour-long Bison Safari tour offered in summer months. A bus takes you into the bison enclosure, where you'll see the animals in their natural habitat. Guides provide information about these majestic giants.

Watch bison wade into a pool to cool off or roll in the dirt to deter biting flies and help shed fur. Bison begin to shed in spring and have ragged patches of old fur until mid-summer. Calves born in spring start out light-coloured and darken as they age. See if you can tell a bison's mood by the swishing of its tale. And be prepared to see one or two relieve themselves. Bison eat grass and poop a lot. You stay on the bus at all times for security reasons, but large windows offer great views. The driver may stop at a safe viewing point and open the front door so passengers can take turns standing on the steps to snap photos without a glass barrier.

As fascinating as the bison are to watch from near or far, you do not want to get in their way. They may be lumbering slowly, but they can run very fast when they choose to. When they move in a group, it is easy to imagine what it must have been like before European settlement, when millions of bison roamed the prairie, creating a thunderous roar with their hooves and causing the earth to shake.

Address 1961 McCreary Road, Winnipeg, MB R3P 2K9, +1 (204) 989-8355, www.fortwhyte.org | Getting there By car, drive west on McGillivray Boulevard, turn north on McCreary Road | Hours See website for seasonal hours | Tip See *Education is the New Bison*, a bison-shaped Val Vint sculpture made of 200 steel replicas of books and articles by Indigenous authors and allies, at Niizhoziibean in The Forks (www.theforks.com).

12 Bois-des-Esprits
Woods where the spirits dwell

Bois-des-Esprits, a pristine urban forest, translates to "woods where the spirits dwell." This forest lives up to its name, as you'll find tree spirits carved into dead trees scattered throughout. Look for a turtle, an owl, doves, human-like faces, and others.

The riverbank forest is an oasis of biodiversity with a variety of plants and wildlife. As you walk amid the shelter of oaks and aspens, listening to the birds and catching glimpses of deer, you'll feel worlds away from the surrounding neighbourhoods. It's a peaceful spot for adults. For children, there are fallen logs to climb, and shelters made of fallen limbs to explore. For young and old, finding tree spirits becomes a treasure hunt. Some carvings are easy to spot. Others require a keener eye. Sometimes you need to look behind you to spot one you missed. All are a delight to discover.

In the early 2000s, the Save Our Seine group and concerned citizens rallied to save the forest from being bulldozed for a housing development. Trails were built in a way to minimize tree damage. In 2006, Walter Mirosh and Robert Leclair carved spirit faces into a three-metre (10-foot) trunk left from a 23-metre (75-foot) tree removed due to Dutch elm disease. The north-facing spirit was named Woody. The spirit facing south received the Ojibwe name Mhitik. Other spirits joined them in 2010, when Murray Watson (1961–2023) began carving smaller spirits in other dead trees.

Although Woody-Mhitik, who sadly succumbed to the elements in 2021, no longer resides in Bois-des-Esprits, well over 20 other tree spirits wait for you. In the summer, canopies of leaves create a shady refuge for your hunt. In the winter, snow carpets the ground, and the frozen Seine River becomes another trail. A reborn Woody-Mhitik lives on at Saint-Boniface Museum, where you'll find a salvaged section of the carving that has been restored by Marcel Ritchot.

TRAVIS SWANN TAYLOR

111
PLACES IN
ATLANTA
THAT YOU
MUST NOT
MISS

KEVSEY ROSS / NINA YEAGER

REVISED 2ND EDITION

111
PLACES IN
AUSTIN
THAT YOU
MUST NOT
MISS

Photographs by Josh Plocher

ALLISON ROBICELLI

REVISED 2ND EDITION

111
PLACES IN
BALTIMORE
THAT YOU
MUST NOT
MISS

Photographs by John Dean

HEATHER KAPPLOW / KIM WINDYKA

111
PLACES IN
BOSTON
THAT YOU
MUST NOT
MISS

Photographs by Alyssa Wood

(111)

111 PLACES
THAT YOU MUST NOT MISS

BRIAN HAYDEN

111
PLACES IN
BUFFALO
THAT YOU
MUST NOT
MISS

Photographs by Jesse Fricke

SAM BIZZARRI

111
PLACES IN
CHICAGO
★★★★
THAT YOU
MUST NOT
MISS

Photographs by Sarah Arnold

PHILIP D. ARMOUR

111
PLACES IN
DENVER
THAT YOU
MUST NOT
MISS

Photographs by Susie Inverso

BRIAN JOSEPH

111
PLACES IN
HOLLYWOOD
THAT YOU
MUST NOT
MISS

DANA DUTERROIL / JOSH FINCHAM

REVISED 4TH EDITION

111
PLACES IN
HOUSTON
THAT YOU
MUST NOT
MISS

Photographs by Daniel Jackson

LAUREL MOGLEN / JULIA POSEY

111
PLACES IN
LOS ANGELES
THAT YOU
MUST NOT
MISS

Photographs by Carolyn Patten

MICHELLE MADDEN

111
PLACES IN
MILWAUKEE
THAT YOU
MUST NOT
MISS

Photographs by Janet McMillan

FLORIANA PETERSEN

111
PLACES IN
NAPA &
SONOMA
THAT YOU
MUST NOT
MISS

Photographs by Steve Werney

JO-ANNE ELIKANN / SUSAN LUSK

111
PLACES IN
NEW YORK
THAT YOU
MUST NOT
MISS

emons

CRISTYLE WOOD EGITTO

111
PLACES IN
PALM BEACH
THAT YOU
MUST NOT
MISS

Photographs by Jakob Takos

(111)

**EXPLORE THE WORLD
RIGHT OUTSIDE YOUR DOOR!**

BRANDON SCHULTZ

111
PLACES IN
PHILADELPHIA
THAT YOU
MUST NOT
MISS

Photographs by Lucy Baber

FLORIANA PETERSEN

111
PLACES IN
SAN FRANCISCO
THAT YOU
MUST NOT
MISS

Photographs by Steve Werney

HARRIET BASKAS

111
PLACES IN
SEATTLE
THAT YOU
MUST NOT
MISS

Photographs by Cortney Kelley

FLORIANA PETERSEN

111
PLACES
IN SILICON
VALLEY
THAT YOU
MUST NOT
MISS

Photographs by Steve Werney

ELIZABETH FOY LARSEN

111
PLACES
IN THE
TWIN CITIES
THAT YOU
MUST NOT
MISS

ANDREA SEIGER

111
PLACES IN
WASHINGTON
THAT YOU
MUST NOT
MISS

Photographs by John Dean

AMY BIZZARRI

111
PLACES FOR
KIDS
IN CHICAGO
THAT YOU
MUST NOT
MISS

DANA DUTERROIL · JONI FINCHAM

111
PLACES FOR
KIDS
IN HOUSTON
THAT YOU
MUST NOT
MISS

EVAN LEVY · RACHEL MAJOR

111
PLACES FOR
KIDS IN
NEW YORK
THAT YOU
MUST NOT
MISS

WENDY LUBOVICH

111
MUSEUMS
IN NEW YORK
THAT YOU
MUST NOT
MISS

This illustrated **111 Places**
guidebook series presents
cities and regions from a
wonderfully different and
personal perspective.

Go off the beaten path
to find the hidden places,
stories, shops, and
neighborhoods that unlock
the true character, history,
and flavor of your home
town or favorite locations
to visit!

@111Places

www.111Places.com

LESLIE ADATTO

111
ROOFTOPS
IN NEW YORK
THAT YOU
MUST NOT
MISS

KAITLIN CALOGERA | REBECCA GRAWL

111
PLACES IN
WOMEN'S
HISTORY
IN WASHINGTON, DC
THAT YOU
MUST NOT
MISS

LAURI WILLIAMSON

111
PLACES IN
BLACK
CULTURE
IN WASHINGTON, DC
THAT YOU
MUST NOT
MISS

JOHN SYKES

111
PLACES
IN LONDON
THAT YOU
SHOULDN'T
MISS

GILLIAN TAIT

111
PLACES IN
EDINBURGH
THAT YOU
SHOULDN'T
MISS

DAVID TAYLOR

111
PLACES IN
THE SCOTTISH
HIGHLANDS
THAT YOU
SHOULDN'T
MISS

Address 650 Shorehill Drive, Winnipeg, MB, www.saveourseine.com/bois-des-esprits |
Getting there Bus 55 to St Anne's & Compark (Stops 50811/50812) | Hours Unrestricted |
Tip Siam Authentic Thai Cuisine is the only Winnipeg Thai restaurant awarded the Royal
Thai Government's "Thai Select Premium" certification for truly authentic Thai cuisine
(587 St Anne's Road, www.siamthairestaurant.ca).

13 Bonnie Day

Cozy bistro with whimsical bathroom art

By day, Bonnie Day is a coffee shop with a friendly, community vibe. In the evening, it becomes a cozy, candlelit bistro. The intimate restaurant serves nourishing comfort food with vegan and gluten-free options for inclusive dining experiences. The best-selling food menu item is Whipped Feta, which also serves as the base for its most popular pizza. The unique cocktail menu is the result of collaboration between bartenders and staff. The wine list features natural, organic, ethically produced wines chosen to pair well with menu options. The walls boast amusing book cover images from the *Library* collection by Michael Dumontier + Neil Farber.

Make sure you visit the accessible bathroom to gaze at the whimsical drawing of Winnipeg landmarks covering two walls. With the artist's permission, co-owner Rachael King, a fan of Marcel Dzama's work, had photographs of his 2007 *Untitled (Winnipeg Map)* made into wallpaper. Dzama's drawings contain fantasy elements and feature humans, animals, and hybrid creatures. Read the brief descriptions that annotate sites in Winnipeg. Creatures hug the Legislative Building and the Royal Canadian Mint. A painting on an easel represents the Winnipeg Art Gallery. The Red River is prominent, too. Items such as the Royal Art Lodge, which he co-founded, reflect Dzama's personal history. Originally from Winnipeg, Dzama now lives in Brooklyn, New York.

Bonnie Day's owners Brian Johnson, Rachael King, and her cousins Jimmy and Hilary King (brother and sister) named the restaurant in honour of their respective uncle and father, who'd cheer "Bonnie Day" when he liked a new idea for the restaurant. Bonnie day means beautiful day in Scotland and also sounds like *bonne idée*, which means good idea in French. If the restaurant had existed in 2007, perhaps Dzama would have thought it a good idea to include Bonnie Day on the map.

Address 898 Westminster Avenue, Winnipeg, MB R3G 1B5, +1 (204) 786-8411, www.bonniedayisagoodidea.ca, hello@bonniedayisagoodidea.ca | Getting there Bus 11 to Portage & Lipton (Stops 10553/10571) | Hours Café Mon–Fri 8am–2pm, Sat & Sun 9am–3pm; restaurant Mon–Sat open at 5pm | Tip The walls of the gender-neutral public washrooms on the second floor of The Forks Market feature artwork by five different local artists (1 Forks Market Road, www.theforks.com).

14 Brookside Cemetery Field of Honour

Honouring their sacrifice

The lane through Brookside Cemetery's Field of Honour weaves through shaded fields with row upon row of stone tombstones in one of Canada's largest and oldest military interment sites.

The Field of Honour opened in 1915 at the request of The Imperial Order Daughters of the Empire (IODE), a charitable organization, to set aside a section for World War I veterans. When it was decided at the end of 1916 that Canadian servicemen with severe wounds or long-term illnesses in British hospitals would be transported back to Canada, Winnipeg became a major treatment centre. The IODE had opened a hospital in 1915, and the national Military Hospitals Commission had established Deer Lodge Hospital in 1916. By the end of the war in 1918, there were six military hospitals and over 900 beds. Most of the men who died from their wounds or illnesses while undergoing treatment in these facilities were buried in Brookside Cemetery. Today, there are over 11,000 graves in the Field of Honour, including over 450 war casualties.

A Cross of Sacrifice war memorial towers in the middle of one section and is dedicated to the memory of those who died in World War I. In another section, you'll find the Commonwealth War Graves Commission Stone of Remembrance, the only one of its kind in Canada. *Their names liveth for evermore*, is etched in the stone. Many grave markers are engraved with the Latin cross. Those of Canadian Army personnel who died during the World Wars and in the post-war era up until 1951 also have a maple leaf. Look for the interpretive panels with information on the grave markers and their restoration.

The Field of Honour, with its memorials and seemingly unending rows of grave markers, is an impressive site evoking a solemn and reflective feeling of awe and appreciation.

Address 3001 Notre Dame Avenue, Winnipeg, MB R3H 1B8, +1 (204) 986-4348, www.winnipeg.ca, cemeteries@winnipeg.ca | Getting there Bus 19, 26, or 77 to Notre Dame & Sherwin (Stops 20038/20039); Field of Honour is in northeast section of cemetery | Hours See website for seasonal hours | Tip The Women's Tribute Memorial Lodge, a 1931 Art Deco veteran's memorial building, is now part of the Movement Disorder Clinic at Deer Lodge Centre (200 Woodlawn Street, www.deerlodge.mb.ca).

15 Bruce D. Campbell Farm & Food Discovery Centre

Learning and fun from the farm to your fork

The first display at the Bruce D. Campbell Farm and Food Discovery Centre welcomes you with a question: "Have you ever wondered where your ice cream or pizza comes from?" Located at the University of Manitoba's Faculty of Agriculture and Food Sciences Glenlea Research Station, the interpretive centre invites visitors of all ages to explore how food is grown, raised, and made in Canada. Come here to learn about agricultural practices, sustainability, Manitoba's soil, and weather.

Interactive exhibits show children the lifecycle of their food from farm to fork. They press buttons to learn why crops grow where they do, follow a maze to answer a true/false question, and lift flaps to learn the time to grow from seed to harvest or which foods are made from wheat. They pretend to work the fields from the inside of a tractor cab. They turn a wheel to grind grain into flour and time how long it takes to clean the udders of a (fake) cow with a spray bottle and rag. Large, colourful displays chart how dairy is processed and answer the question "Where does all the poop go?"

Four windows in the interpretive centre provide views into a working pig barn. Weather permitting, you can book a tour of a state-of-the-art dairy cattle barn and a chicken barn. Interpretive centres attached to the barns offer even more information. Through the window into the cattle barn, you can watch the "robot" milking machine at work. Rows of hens (real) sit behind windows in the egg centre. Another window allows you views of people sorting and packing eggs.

There will be times, particularly June, when the centre is very busy with school tours, and you may not be able to book a barn tour. But you can always explore on your own and discover many wonderful things about the food you eat.

Address 1290 Research Station Road, Glenlea, MB R0G 0S0, +1 (204) 883-2524, www.umanitoba.ca/farm-and-food-discovery-centre, ffdc@umanitoba.ca | Getting there By car, drive south on Highway 75, turn east at Research Road | Hours Tue–Sat 10am–4pm | Tip Take a gentle scenic nature walk on the St. Adolphe Friendship Trail located along a migratory bird flight path (west end of St. Paul Street, St. Adolphe).

16   Buhler Gallery

The healing power of art

You may be surprised to find an art gallery at one of Winnipeg's hospitals. Galerie Buhler Gallery at St. Boniface Hospital was the first hospital art gallery in Manitoba and one of only a few in Canada. It opened in 2007, thanks to a generous donation from philanthropists John and Bonnie Buhler. As per the gallery's website, St. Boniface Hospital "recognizes the benefits of the arts in health and healing, and its impact on the fabric of daily life and the community as a whole."

The gallery is a tranquil and welcoming space. Bright white walls and alcoves provide a showcase for the art, and benches and chairs invite you to linger. Volunteers and visitors occasionally play the grand piano donated by Dr. Brendan MacDougall.

The gallery stages three to five curated exhibitions and one community show a year and features the works of contemporary Canadian artists, many from Manitoba and the prairie provinces. Their varied work includes printmaking, painting, photography, craft, drawing, and multi-media art. Shows spotlight one or two artists or sometimes multiple artists around a particular theme. One show contained cell phone photos taken by hospital staff, physicians, and volunteers of something they wanted to share about their day. The gallery will partner with rural arts organizations for its community show. And its own collection of over 450 donated artworks are displayed throughout the hospital.

A tangible recognition of the integral part art plays in health and well-being, Galerie Buhler Gallery is accessed from the Everett Atrium, the hospital's main entrance. Admission is free. Staff, volunteers, patients, and hospital visitors find the gallery to be a place of serenity and respite, as well as a place to appreciate the art. The gallery is open to the general public and aims to be "a place of hope, healing, and contemplation for all who visit."

Address 409 Taché Avenue, Winnipeg, MB R2H 2A6, www.galeriebuhlergallery.ca, tgadd@sbgh.mb.ca | Getting there Bus 10 to Taché & Rinella (Stop 50952) or Taché & Dollard (Stop 50199) | Hours Mon–Fri 10am–5pm, Sat 10am–4pm, Sun noon–4pm | Tip Belvédère Saint-Boniface on Taché Promenade offers great views of the river, The Forks, the Canadian Museum for Human Rights, and the Winnipeg skyline (Taché Avenue across from the Saint-Boniface Museum).

17 Buller Cairn
An unlikely tombstone

A simple cairn in front of the Buller Building on the University of Manitoba's Fort Garry campus commemorates its namesake, pioneering botanist Arthur Henry Reginald Buller. The cairn also contains an urn with his ashes. Buller was one of the University's first six science professors hired in 1904. He specialized in fungi and wheat rust. His research led to the 1925 founding of the federally funded Dominion Rust Research Laboratory to combat agricultural crop diseases.

In a 2004 article for the Manitoba Historical Society, scientist-historian Gordon Goldsborough writes about Buller's career, life, and relationship with the University. A spellbinding lecturer, Buller felt strongly about the important role of research at a university. His own research gained international recognition, and he received many awards and honorary degrees. He gave public lectures. He wrote poetry and was known as the Poet Scientist. He never married. Although he invested in residential properties, his own Winnipeg home was a cheap hotel.

Certain events in the 1930s led to his estrangement from the university. He, along with other senior professors, reluctantly accepted a year's leave of absence to save the university costs. But the frequent streetcar travel between a new science building at the Fort Garry campus and his Broadway office led to his resignation from teaching. When asked to vacate his office space in 1942, he refused the offer of space elsewhere and wrote a poem about his figurative death.

Buller died in 1944, but his ashes were not placed beneath this cairn until 2013. They'd been at the Rust Laboratory from his death until the laboratory closed. Given his role in developing the university's research-based science teaching program, it seems fitting that his ashes would reside on campus. But you have to wonder how he would feel about it being his final resting place....

...THUR HENRY MºG..ALD ...
...s born in Birmingham, Engl..., ...
...e University of London (189...), ...
...zig (Ph.D. 1899), Munich and ...
...-1903), before coming to Winnipeg ...
...936, when he retired (as Profess...
...us - the study of the higher fung..., ...
...sident (1927/28) and Flavelle Medal (1929). ...
...7), honorary doctorates from Manitoba (1924) ...
...nia (1938). An outstanding teacher and ...
...y's problems, including the inadequacy of ...
...obbles: billiards and crossing the Atlantic (65 times). He ...

Buller's urn was enclosed
in this monument in 2013.

Address 45 Chancellors Circle, Winnipeg, MB R3T 2N2, +1 (800) 432-1960,
www.umanitoba.ca | Getting there Bus BLUE, 47, 60, 74, 75, 78, 662, 671, or 672 to
U of M | Hours Unrestricted | Tip The Buller Greenhouse, a rare educational greenhouse
with a diverse plant collection, is open to the public at set times (45 Chancellors Circle,
www.umanitoba.ca).

18___C2 Centre for Craft
Honouring the handmade

C2 Centre for Craft, a shared initiative of the Manitoba Craft Council (MCC) and the Manitoba Crafts Museum and Library (MCML), showcases the best of handmade craft artistry in Manitoba. MCC provides support to craft media artists, and MCML preserves historical and contemporary craft.

Canada's only museum of craft has a strong textile base, including quilts and embroidery. But its collection of 11,000 pieces also features ceramics, glassware, beaded work, jewelry, and more, all with a Manitoba connection. A bright gallery space hosts exhibitions curated by both MCC and MCML that feature pieces from the museum's collections, works by contemporary artists, and occasionally items from other museums. Exhibitions change several times per year, so your visits will always be new and different. A 2023 exhibition in collaboration with Ross House Museum that featured Indigenous beadwork, embroidery, and quillwork from museums throughout Manitoba won a Governor General's History Award for Excellence in Museums.

In a display hallway behind the main exhibition space, you'll see items from the museum's own collection. This display changes yearly. An attractive shop sells a curated selection of handmade pieces by emerging and established craft artists working in a variety of mediums.

At the back, you'll find the inviting Gladys Chown Memorial Library, whose shelves house a variety of craft publications from how-to books to books about specific crafts to illustrated art books. As many as 20 to 30 per cent of the books would not be found in any other library. Books from all eras show how craft has evolved over the years. Anyone can read the books at the C2 Centre, but you must be a member to check one out.

If the crafts on display and for sale inspire you to try your own hand at making something, you might want to look into the workshops offered by both MCC and MCML at C2 Centre for Craft.

Address Suite 1-329 Cumberland Avenue, Winnipeg, MB R3B 1T2, +1 (204) 615-3951, https://c2centreforcraft.ca, info@c2centreforcraft.ca | Getting there Bus 17 to Notre Dame & Hargrave (Stop 10766) or bus 66 to Donald & Notre Dame (Stop 10667) | Hours Wed–Sat noon–4pm | Tip The Stoneware Gallery is one of the longest existing cooperatively managed and artist-run pottery shops in Canada (778 Corydon Avenue, www.stonewaregallery.com).

19 Canadian Plains Gallery

Indigenous fine art

The luxurious, Beaux-Art-style Canadian Pacific Railway Station that once saw thousands of immigrants pass through it is now the Neeginan Centre housing several Indigenous organizations. A shop on the main floor next to what was the railway's grand waiting room boasts an amazing collection of high-quality Indigenous art, 90 per cent of which is created by Manitoba artists.

Paintings on the walls of Canadian Plains Gallery include classic works by well-known Indigenous artists, as well as pieces by the new and up-and-coming. Bins contain a large selection of shrink-wrapped works. Free-standing, revolving racks hold cards and prints. Carvings of all kinds, including soapstone, sit in display cases, and you'll see dream catchers and jewelry as well. Among the diversity of mediums, you may find beadwork, porcupine quill work, deerskin painting, caribou hair tufting, birch bark biting, pottery, and wood burning.

In 1995, gallery founder Jacques St. Goddard worked at the Aboriginal Arts Council while taking artist management training. He organized art shows and powwows. He'd been slated to work at the council, but it had been dissolved by the time he graduated. So he took a summer job working in northern communities and reserves with the Manitoba Arts Council. He then leased space and used the community connections he'd made to open Canadian Plains Gallery, offering Indigenous artists a place to sell their works at a fair price with minimal commissions. Today, the gallery continues to promote the highest quality of Indigenous art, and St. Goddard helps artists with portfolio development. They also provide photography services and can arrange dance demonstrations.

St. Goddard says respect for the artists and respect for the culture is at the core of the fine art gallery. He also says that every piece of artwork has a story or a teaching with a connection to Mother Earth.

Address 106–181 Higgins Avenue, Winnipeg, MB R3B 3G1, +1 (204) 943-4972, www.canadianplainsgallery.com, cpgallery@gmail.com | Getting there Bus 44 or 47 to Higgins & Maple (Stops 10353/10368) | Hours Mon–Fri 9:30am–4:30pm; by appointment on weekends | Tip Find Indigenous-made jewelry, clothing, accessories, home décor, and more at Anishinaabe Girl Boutique (165 Lilac Street, www.anishinaabegirl.com).

20   Carol Shields Labyrinth

King Park memorial to a beloved author

What is a fitting memorial to an author? In Carol Shields' book, *Larry's Party*, an ordinary man learns to make the garden mazes he loves. He also creates a labyrinth. So, her fans created a labyrinth in King Park in her honour.

Unlike a maze in which you can get lost in pathways with dead ends, there is only one path through a labyrinth. It winds back and forth to the centre and spirals back out again. Walking a labyrinth is said to awaken the right brain and release intuition and creativity. The Carol Shields Memorial Labyrinth's packed gravel path winds through stone-edged flower beds. The mix of stone and flowers reflects themes from her book *The Stone Diaries*. Many of the plants, such as daisies, crocuses, and spirea, are recurring themes in Shields' books. The Meditation / Healing Garden, featuring Indigenous herbs, was inspired by her dignity while dealing with breast cancer.

Interpretive signage provides information about labyrinths and Carol Shields (1935 – 2003).

Shields grew up in Chicago and lived most of her adult life in Winnipeg. She wrote 10 novels and produced many other literary works, in which she mostly wrote about the lives of women. Her novels were often set close to Winnipeg and have been published in 27 languages. *The Stone Diaries* won both the Governor General's Award for Literature and the Pulitzer Prize. Two stone walls near the entrance contain quotes from her works.

Signage says there is no one correct way to walk the labyrinth – you simply enter it and allow the pathway to take you to the centre. Some people take a question or prayer with them and allow the labyrinth to open up possibilities. A bench in the centre allows time for reflection. Follow the same pathway back out or take the short path through the Meditation Garden. Whichever way you walk the labyrinth, you are likely to feel a sense of peace, calm, and quiet stillness.

Address 198 King's Drive, Winnipeg, MB, www.mhs.mb.ca/docs/sites/shieldslabyrinth.shtml | Getting there Bus 662, 671, or 672 to Silverstone & King's Drive (Stops 60085/60086) | Hours Daily 7am–10pm | Tip Check out the bright red Chinese pagoda beside the lake in another part of King's Park (198 King's Drive, parkmaps.winnipeg.ca).

21 Caron Park

A farm and ferry crossing once stood here

A bench in Caron Park overlooks the Assiniboine River, and the placard beside it explains the place's historical significance. The St. Charles Ferry operated here from 1908 until 1959, when the Perimeter Highway Bridge was built. The ferry connected Charleswood on the south side of the river with St. Charles on the north, making it crucial for commerce, church, school, and family and social visits. As you look across the river to the north, you see the buildings of St. Charles Roman Catholic Church, built in 1929, and St. Charles Catholic School, which dates to 1906.

From 1870 to 1908, the ferry operated at a spot to the east known as The Passage, which was a historic river crossing for herds of bison. First Nations peoples, fur traders, and settlers also crossed here. But the shallow water that made for a good ford caused problems for ferry service. So, the ferry moved west to where the Caron family had built a ferry crossing to get their produce across the river to St. Charles and the Portage Trail.

The 20-acre Caron Park was created in 1980 on land that once belonged to the Caron family, who had begun farming in the area in 1880. Their farm had a large barn, a cheese factory, a blacksmith shop, and a windmill for pumping water. In 1905, the Carons built a large, two-and-a-half storey, Queen Anne-style house. When the park was created, the Charleswood Historical Society undertook preservation of the house to save it from demolition, and the restored house now stands in the middle of the park. It remains a private residence and is viewable from the exterior only. Look for interpretive signage near the house to learn its history.

The old Baie St. Paul Road, which ran through riverside bush from St. Boniface to Baie St. Paul, crossed this site. Walk five minutes west to see the deep tracks left by the Red River Carts that transported goods along the route.

Address 50 Cass Street, Winnipeg, MB R3R 3C7, parkmaps.winnipeg.ca | Getting there Bus 66 to Roblin & Barker (Stop 60573) or Roblin & Dale (Stop 60574) | Hours Unrestricted | Tip Among the artifacts at Charleswood Museum, you'll find an original wooden ferry pulley and an old map showing Baie St. Paul Road (5006 Roblin Boulevard, www.charleswoodhistoricalsociety.ca/charleswood-museum).

22 CESB Ice Climbing Tower

Bringing the mountain to the city

You may not expect to find ice climbing in a mountainless city, but every winter, Club d'escalade de Saint-Boniface (CESB), the Saint Boniface Section of The Alpine Club of Canada, brings the mountain to Winnipeg with the creation of a 20-metre-high (65.6-foot-high), freestanding ice tower. First built in 1996, North America's original ice tower resembles a frozen waterfall and offers ice climbing opportunities to both club and non-club members.

The wood and steel structure that forms the base of the tower is used in summer for rock climbing. It takes about 200 volunteer hours to plug the climbing holds and ready the tower for winter flooding. Water is then run over the tower for 7 to 14 days. Working across three shifts a day, volunteers constantly monitor this process and adjust water flow and pressure to account for temperature and wind direction, so the full length of the tower freezes fairly evenly. It then becomes smoother over time, though natural pockets develop where people have placed their feet. The ice tower is a fascinating sight when people are scaling its sides, and it is impressive to see even without climbers.

If you'd like to try ice climbing, the tower is open for public climbing on Saturdays – no training or prior experience is necessary. Trained volunteers set you up and provide instruction. Climbers wear a harness attached to a rope, so when you reach the top or are ready to come back down, that rope is used to lower you safely to the ground. There is a charge for the climb, but harnesses, helmets, ice tools, boots, and crampons are available free of charge. Climbing during the rest of the week is available only to club members. The length of the ice climbing season depends on the weather, and it typically runs from early to mid-January until mid-March. You can also go summer rock climbing on Wednesdays from June through September.

Address 141 Messager Street, Winnipeg, MB R2H, www.cesb.club, cesb.club@gmail.com | Getting there Bus 10 or 43 to Provencher & Taché (Stops 50176/50177) | Hours Seasonally Sat 9:30am–4pm | Tip For winter fun at ground level, try cross-country skiing at Windsor Park Nordic Centre, where rental equipment and lessons are available (10 Des Meurons Street, www.windsorparknordic.ca).

23   Chaeban Ice Cream

Winnipeggers eat ice cream in the winter too

Who opens an ice cream shop in Winnipeg on December 21? Joseph Chaeban, his wife Zainab Ali, and business partner Darryl Stewart did just that in 2017 on a -20°C day, and customers showed up.

Joseph, a second-generation cheese maker and dairy scientist, and Zainab had recently moved from Ontario to Winnipeg in 2015 when the South Osborne community sponsored Zainab's family, Syrian refugees living in dangerous conditions across Lebanon and Turkey, to come to Canada. The couple opened the ice cream shop as a way to say thank you and to create employment opportunities for Zainab's family.

Chaeban purchases raw milk, does its own pasteurization, and uses all natural ingredients in its more than a dozen flavours, though the dairy-free flavours use a coconut or almond base.

Their Salty Carl flavor, featuring sea-salted caramel, was the Grand Champion, the best in Canada, at Toronto's 2022 Royal Agricultural Winter Fair, the largest agricultural and equestrian fair in the world. Rocky Ricardo placed first in the chocolate category, and Prairie Berry flavor placed fifth in Canada in the "Other Flavour" category. Abir Al Sham, a take on a traditional Syrian recipe made with rose water, orange blossom water, toasted pistachios and cashews, ricotta cheese, and orchid root powder, placed sixth.

Chaeban returned to his cheese-making roots during the tough times of COVID-19 shutdowns. The cheeses, which include both creamy and firm fetas, ricotta, mascarpone, halloumi, and labneh, can be found in major stores across Western Canada. Four, including both fetas, placed in the top 10 at the 2023 Royal.

At Chaeban, ice cream is served in cones or bowls. If you can't decide on a flavour, try a flight of four. Unlike most Winnipeg ice cream shops, which shut down for the winter, Chaeban is open year-round. In the winter you may want to try the hot chocolate infused with ice cream.

Address 390 Osborne Street, Winnipeg, MB R3L 1Z9, +1 (204) 475-6226,
www.chaebanicecream.com, events@chaebanicecream.com | Getting there Bus 16 to
Osborne & Woodward (Stop 10002) or Osborne & Glasgow (Stop 10064) | Hours
Daily noon–10pm | Tip Black Market Provisions nearby sells a curated collection
of gifts, housewares, trinkets, pantry provisions and house-made food (550 Osborne
Street, www.blackmarketwpg.com).

24 Chinatown Arch Gate

Crossing a once-bustling community

A Chinese-style upturned roof, red trim, and Chinese lettering make the decorative bridge crossing King Street a recognizable symbol for the neighbourhood. Chinatown Arch Gate, which opened in 1987, connects the Dynasty Building and the Mandarin Building. In 2013, the street bridge even appeared on a Canadian stamp as one of Canada Post's eight new stamps commemorating gates across the country.

The gate was built at the same time as the Dynasty Building, part of an area revitalization. The distinctive Dynasty incorporates elements of traditional Chinese architecture and houses the Winnipeg Chinese Cultural and Community Centre, as well as other businesses and offices. Its many roofs are a symbol of good luck. The Mandarin Building on the other side of the bridge dates to the 1880s, when it served as Winnipeg Police Court. Chinese influences were added during a renovation in the 1980s. The exterior side facing King Street features a colourful, ceramic replica of the *Nine Imperial Dragons* mural found in Beijing.

Railway construction brought Chinese immigrants to the prairies in the late 1800s, and Chinatown developed in the early 1900s just outside Winnipeg's central business district. As the Chinese population grew, this part of town became the centre of life for the Chinese community. By the 1960s, the majority of the residents lived in other areas, but Chinatown remained an important shopping and cultural hub. Today, Chinatown is not as vibrant, but you'll find a number of Chinese restaurants and stores north of Chinatown Arch Gate.

In front of the Dynasty Building, look for a small garden of Chinese design. The Chinese Heritage Garden includes ponds, pagodas, and a zig-zag bridge. It bustles during events staged by the Winnipeg Chinese Cultural and Community Centre, but at other times is a tranquil place to sit, reflect, and view the Chinatown Arch Gate.

Address 180 King Street, Winnipeg, MB R3B 3G8 | Getting there Bus 11, 15, 16, 18, 20, 21, 24, 44, 45, or 47 to Main & James (Stops 10629/10634) | Hours Unrestricted | Tip The banquet-sized Kum Koon Garden Restaurant offers Winnipeg's longest-running *dim sum* service (257 King Street, www.kumkoongarden.com).

25 Chocolatier Constance Popp

Telling stories with artisan chocolate

You'll enjoy browsing Chocolatier Constance Popp's attractive display of artisan chocolate products almost as much as you'll savour the tastes. Admire the pretty bonbons, premium bars, and chocolate treats in a variety of shapes. The shop's signature items, such as chocolate puffs, are available year-round. Other products and designs change with the seasons. At any one time, you'll find about 100 different products made with premium chocolate and other whole-food ingredients, and no preservatives or artificial flavours.

Owner Constance Menzies began making chocolates as a hobby while working as an environmental technologist. Her passion evolved into a new career when she opened her first store in 2007. She was Manitoba's first bean-to-bar maker, and bean-to-bar chocolate now makes up about 20 per cent of her offerings. Menzies has supplied chocolates for the Golden Globes, the Oscars, the Junos, and Royal visits.

Her artistic eye and knack for connecting flavours lead to unique offerings. The Birch Bark Bar features birch syrup and is made in a special mold created from a chunk of birch bark. Nine iconic Winnipeg buildings form the design on the Winnipeg Chocolate Bar. The word "Winnipeg" appears in the font the city used when it was first incorporated. Other chocolate shapes include a Manitoba map, a bison, the Golden Boy statue, the Canadian Museum for Human Rights, and a high-heeled shoe. The popular, dark chocolate "Manitobar" is filled with hemp, sunflower seeds, flax seed, gianduja chocolate, and praline. Colourfully decorated bonbons contain a variety of fillings.

Sit at a table and enjoy a cup of coffee or a chocolate drink. Depending on the day, you can get a creamy thick milk chocolate, or a spicy rich chocolate beverage made with dark chocolate, almond milk, vanilla, cinnamon, and hot pepper based on an original Yucatán recipe.

Address 180 Provencher Boulevard, Winnipeg, MB R2H 0G3, +1 (204) 897-0689, www.constancepopp.com | Getting there Bus 10 or 43 to Provencher & St. Joseph (Stops 50174/50175) | Hours Mon–Fri 10am–5pm, Sat 10am–4pm | Tip Visit Fromagerie Bothwell for award-winning Manitoba Bothwell cheese and other culinary products from the province (136 Provencher Boulevard, www.fromageriebothwell.ca).

26 Cleocatra Cafe

Play with cats in a cozy coffee shop

Cleocatra Cafe (or Quán Che Phê) is not just a coffee shop. It's also a cat café, where you can watch, play, and cuddle with adorable kitties.

Vintage decor fills the front part of the shop, and Tiffany lamps hang from the ceiling. Antique cabinet sewing machines serve as tables. Dictionary prints, created by an artist in Poland and framed with window frames from abandoned houses, cover the walls. You'll want to linger in the fun atmosphere here, but cat lovers will want to leave the front room to get beyond the glass wall and door and into the back room because the back room is all about the cats.

Cats run and climb on vintage furniture, cat chairs, and cat ladders. They curl up in cat beds. Human visitors, who need to book in advance, are given a treat to take to the cats and a craft set to build at home or at the café.

Cleocatra's owners came from Vietnam, where they saw dogs, cats, and rabbits being treated poorly. They wanted to do more to save abandoned cats and partnered with the non-profit Trails of Freedom Rescue. All cats at Cleocatra come from the Winnipeg-based shelter. The number of cats in the back room at any one time varies, and you may meet as many as 20.

A chalkboard at the café's entrance states how many cats are currently in residence. Should you become enamored with a particular animal, you can arrange an adoption. Photos of cats that have been adopted are posted in the front room.

The café offers espresso-based coffees, tea, smoothies, and a selection of desserts. It also serves Vietnamese coffee, which comes with a dripper. In Vietnamese culture, as you wait for the coffee to drip through the traditional *phin* filter into a cup that may already contain condensed milk, you take time to savour the moment and to chat with friends. Cleocatra encourages chatting among the people as well as interaction between people and cats.

Address 859 Portage Avenue, Winnipeg, MB R3G 0N8, +1 (204) 772-5410, www.cleocatracafe.ca, info@cleocatracafe.ca | Getting there Bus 11 to Portage & Simcoe (Stop 10551) or bus 11, 21, or 24 to Portage & Burnell (Stop 10552) or Portage & Arlington (Stop 10573) | Hours Cafe: Mon–Thu 11am–9pm, Fri–Sun 9am–10pm; Cat Room: reservations required | Tip The *Table of Contents* public art piece in Vimy Ridge Memorial Park features phrases supplied by community residents inscribed in an aluminum table and bench, including "I Can Breathe Here" (821 Preston Avenue, parkmaps.winnipeg.ca).

27 Cooks Creek Grotto
Healing powers of Lourdes in Manitoba

You may do a double take when you first glimpse a large, U-shaped structure in the middle of a flat field alongside Route 212 in Cooks Creek. Its grey walls look like they're made of rock. This is the Grotto of Our Lady of Lourdes, modelled after the Our Lady of Lourdes Grotto in Lourdes, France, where Bernadette first saw apparitions of the Virgin Mary in 1858.

Two long walls slope up around the lawn to the open grotto, and a large crucifix with statues of mourners at its base sits on the lawn area in front of the grotto. Step inside the grotto area to see statues of the Virgin Mary and St. Bernadette resting in nooks in the wall. Cave-like doorways at the back open into small side-rooms, where you'll find altars containing statues representing the Stations of the Cross, labelled in both Ukrainian and English. On top of the grotto is a platform, where an empty cross, flanked by Canadian and Ukrainian flags, tops the structure.

The grotto belongs to Immaculate Conception Church, the adjacent, onion-domed building elaborately painted in the blue and yellow colours of the Ukrainian flag. Built almost entirely by hand by volunteers over two decades starting in 1930, it is one of the largest Ukrainian churches in Western Canada and a National Historic Site.

Cooks Creek Grotto was the vision of parish priest Philip Ruh (1883–1962) as a spiritual centre of Canada. Construction began in 1954, and he would not live to see it completed over the following several years.

The Grotto and grounds are visible year-round, and you can take a tour of the church and Grotto on weekends from the end of May to the end of October. You are free to wander through the Grotto as you wish, exploring the "caves," studying the sculptures, and maybe even finding spiritual solace. Ramps lead to platform areas that provide great views of the surrounding, peaceful countryside.

Address 68003 Cooks Creek Road, Cooks Creek, MB R5M 0E2, +1 (204) 444-2478, www.facebook.com/icccookscreek | Getting there By car, drive north on Highway 59, east on Provincial Road 213, and north on Provincial Road 212 (Cook's Creek Road) | Hours Tours May–Oct Sat & Sun noon–6pm or by reservation | Tip View the collection of artifacts dedicated to Slavic pioneers at Cooks Creek Heritage Museum, founded by Father Alois Krivanek (1919–2009), known as the "junk priest" (68148 Cooks Creek Road, www.cchm.ca).

28 __ Cornish Library
Elegant library with a not-so-elegant namesake

The century-old Cornish Library in Armstrong's Point retains its original charm and exudes a quiet elegance, something that cannot be attributed to its namesake, Frances Evans Cornish, Winnipeg's first mayor.

One of three Carnegie libraries built in Winnipeg, its brick exterior with Tuscan stone columns at the entrance looks much like it did when the library opened in 1915. The welcoming, open-area space inside with extensive restored woodwork feels both new and old. Atop the entryway, a wooden-spindle-railed balcony, which may once have been the librarian's office, overlooks the entire main floor. Fireplaces remain, although non-functional. The painting *Our Cornish Library and the Suffrage Saga* by Naomi Gerrard hangs over one fireplace to honour suffragists who once met in the basement, including Martha Jane Hample (1859–1927) and Nellie McClung (1873–1951). A library renovation, completed in 2021, added a beautiful, glass-paned reading room at the back of the library. Sitting a storey above ground, the space looks out over the river.

Frances Evans Cornish has been described as a belligerent, bigoted drunk. *One Great History*, a podcast about the great (and not so great) history of Winnipeg, recounts how Cornish, shortly after arriving in Winnipeg in 1872, became involved in a federal election riot in which newspaper offices were ransacked and a polling book was burned. He became mayor in 1874, after winning the election with 383 votes to his opponent's 178. There were only 388 registered voters, but Cornish exploited a loophole giving property owners one vote for each property they owned. After his term as mayor, he was elected to the provincial Legislature and at one time appointed alderman. His outrageous behaviour continued. He picked fights, called a fellow alderman a dog, and was kicked out of the Legislature for a lengthy nearly disgraceful speech.

Address 20 West Gate, Winnipeg, MB R3C 2E1, +1 (204) 986-4680, wpl.winnipeg.ca/library | Getting there Bus 20 or 29 to Maryland & Misericordia Health Centre (Stop 10815) or bus 20, 29, or 635 to Sherbrook & West Gate (Stop 10190) | Hours See website for hours | Tip For a hearty breakfast or classic diner meal, visit The Nook, a cozy old-school diner with a colourful mural about the eatery's history on an outside wall (43 Sherbrook Street).

29 Coronation Bowling Centre

Decades of bowling history on these lanes

There is a warm, homey feel in the Coronation Bowling Centre. A community staple, the venue hosts regular daily and nightly leagues. Families come to spend time together. Local schools bring their students on outings, and the centre hosts birthday parties and corporate team-building events. Its eight bowling lanes have seen decades of bowling. They are the last wooden bowling lane floors left in Manitoba and were laid board by board when the centre was built.

When Mr. M. Sigurdson opened the centre in 1948, it offered three floors of ten-pin and five-pin bowling. A newspaper article about the opening said "those who know" claimed it was the finest in Canada. At the time, the pins were set by pin boys. In 1960, Sigurdson installed automatic pinsetters, the first in Manitoba. With that technological advancement, the centre became solely a five-pin bowling alley. The basement has served as a dance studio since the 1980s, and a fitness centre opened on the top floor in 2010.

Sigurdson sold Coronation in 1966, and it changed hands a couple of times after that. The Llewellyn family has owned it since 1997. Sheila Llewellyn had worked at the lanes since 1968 when she started answering phones here. Today, you'll find her daughter Dawn and son Jim at the centre, working, greeting newcomers and regulars alike.

In 2019, Coronation became the first sensory certified bowling centre in Canada. Staff have been trained to serve guests with sensory needs and can provide them with noise-cancelling headphones, fidget tools, verbal cue cards, and weighted lap pads.

You can try bumper bowling, glow bowling on black-lit lanes, and Bingo Bowl, where bowlers play to a Bingo card, as well as traditional five-pin. And enjoy pizza, hamburgers, hot dogs, fries, jungle fries, and chicken wraps, and maybe a bowling-themed cocktail.

Address 255 Taché Avenue, Winnipeg, MB R2H 1Z8, +1 (204) 237-8684, www.5pin.ca, bowling@5pin.ca | Getting there Bus 10 to Taché & Eugenie (Stops 50204/50205) or bus 14 or 55 to St. Mary's & Enfield (Stops 50266/50267) | Hours Mon–Thu noon–4pm & 6–10pm, Fri noon–4pm & 6pm–midnight, Sat noon–midnight, Sun noon–8pm | Tip Visit the Belgian Club on Tuesday evenings to try your hand at Belgian bowling, similar to boules but with wheel-shaped balls (407 Provencher Boulevard, www.belgianclub.ca).

30 _Crokicurl at The Forks

Where curling meets crokinole

When you visit The Forks in winter, you'll find an octagonal-shaped ice rink in the plaza in front of The Forks Market. Red, white, and blue concentric circles emanating from its centre resemble a curling house. The octagonal shape, eight posts placed around the outside of the inner red circle, and an indentation at its very centre remind you of the game of crokinole. This is crokicurl, a combination of crokinole and curling.

Crokinole is a Canadian board game in which players use their fingers and thumbs to flick wooden discs toward the centre of a wooden board, and points are awarded based on how close the disc gets to the centre. The sport of curling is a popular winter pastime in Winnipeg. Players on two opposing teams take turns sliding granite stones down a sheet of ice toward the "house," marked by painted concentric circles, at the other end.

Crokicurl, invented by Public City Architecture, was first played at The Forks in 2017. Since then, it has appeared in several Canadian cities. It is played with two teams, composed of one to two players each. Each team has four rocks weighing 20 pounds each, or roughly half the weight of a normal curling stone. Players slide the rocks toward the centre. The object of the game is to accumulate the most points by positioning the rocks to stop in the highest scoring circles, similar to crokinole. Teams attempt to knock opponents' rocks out of play and keep their own rocks in the scoring circles. Rules are posted at the site.

Rocks for playing crokicurl at The Forks are available on a first-come, first-served basis. The Forks requests that visitors be respectful of other players and limit playing time to one hour. One of The Forks blog posts about the game recommends that the losing team treat the winning team to mini donuts, a cinnamon bun, or a round of drinks from The Common in The Forks Market.

Address 1 Forks Market Road, Winnipeg, MB R3C 4L8, www.theforks.com, info@theforks.com | Getting there Bus 38 to Forks Market (Stop 10907) | Hours Unrestricted in season | Tip Visit Across the Board Game Café for food, drink, and a game of crokinole, one of the more than 1,600 titles in its game library (105 – 211 Bannatyne Avenue, www.acrosstheboardcafe.com).

31 Dave Barber Cinematheque
Screening the best of independent cinema

Visit the 85-seat Dave Barber Cinematheque theatre for a unique film-viewing experience. Enjoy the best of Canadian and world cinema in a comfortable, intimate space offering up-close and personal movie-watching with a sense of community. Many screenings include panel discussions, post-film Q&As, or special introductions, as well as locally made short films.

Part of the Winnipeg Film Group, Dave Barber Cinematheque features a wide variety of films, including award-winning international films, Canadian independent movies, documentaries, cult classics, restored older films, and more. The theatre focuses on independent films and highlights Winnipeg filmmakers and underrepresented artists. It is the place to see the films you won't see at the mainstream theatre chains. Examples of special screening series include Trash Cult Tuesdays with screenings of cheap cult classic films, and a monthly Astral Projection series exploring astrology through film. Cinematheque runs a documentary festival in November and December. Together with the Winnipeg Architecture Foundation, it hosts an annual architecture and design film festival. The movie house can run 16mm and 35mm film projections, as well as digital projection. Popcorn, snacks, and beverages – including wine, beer, and coolers – are available.

The Winnipeg Film Group formed in 1974, and its Cinematheque program began in 1982. In 1986, Cinematheque moved to its current location in the Artspace Building. The theatre was renamed after the 2021 death of Dave Barber, the theatre's programmer since its inception and an important figure in the development of Winnipeg's independent cinema.

The non-profit, artist-run theatre is Winnipeg's only independent movie theatre and the only movie theatre in the downtown area. It is a place for cinephiles, filmmakers, nostalgia seekers, and anyone who just wants to see a good movie.

Address 100 Arthur Street, Winnipeg, MB R3B 1H3, +1 (204) 925-3456, www.davebarbercinematheque.com, cinematheque@winnipegfilmgroup.com | Getting there Bus 11, 15, 16, 18, 20, 21, 24, 44, 45, or 47 to Main & McDermot (Stops 10628/ 10636), or Main & Lombard (Stop 10637) | Hours See website for schedule | Tip The Costume Museum of Canada reflects Canada's history through dress via rotating displays in their office space and during special exhibits (410–70 Arthur Street, www.costumemuseumofcanada.com).

32 Dino's Grocery Mart
Around the world in a single grocery store

A walk through Dino's Grocery Mart is a world culinary tour. Known as the largest international grocery store in the province, Dino's carries East Indian, Pakistani, Bangladeshi, Sri Lankan, Caribbean, Middle Eastern, African, Asian, and South and Central American foods.

In the fresh produce aisle you'll find common North American fruit and vegetables, but you'll also find dasheen, cassava, eddoes, African yams, dragon fruit, sugar cane, and more. There are numerous types of rice, flours, and beans, an extensive collection of hot sauces, an array of spices, and dried chilies. In the bread section, you'll find rotis, tortillas, hard dough bread, Ethiopian flatbread, cassava bread, coco bread, and Canadian breads. You'll also find Lagos Loaf, a version of the soft, dense, sweet, white Agege bread originating in Lagos, Nigeria and made in Winnipeg by Arabelle's Bakery. Products, grouped on shelves by type of cuisine, include raw ingredients for ethnic dishes, as well as prepared foods to heat and serve with minimal effort. Freezers contain all kinds of meat, fish, and packaged foods. The store carries kitchenware items and beauty products, including a large hair section for people of colour.

Dinu "Dino" Tailor arrived in Canada in 1974. Working as an accountant for a grocery business while studying sparked a desire to own his own grocery business. He purchased an Indian grocery store and officially established Dino's Grocery Mart in 1982. Initially, he stocked mostly Indian products, but over time, he added items from other nationalities as requested by customers. The store has expanded and moved locations twice since it opened. Dino's continues to source products to satisfy customer requests.

Whether you want to recreate the flavours of home, prepare an ethnic feast, or expand your culinary horizons, Dino's is the place to go for the ingredients.

Address 84 Isabel Street, Winnipeg, MB R3A 1E9, +1 (204) 942-1526, www.dinosgrocerymart.com, info@dinosgrocerymart.com | Getting there Bus 17 or 33 or 38 to Isabel & Bannatyne (Stop 10753), bus 33 or 38 to Isabel & McDermot (Stops 10752), or bus 17 to McDermot & Isabel (Stop 10773) | Hours Mon–Sat 9:30am–8pm, Sun 11:30am–5pm | Tip De Luca's Specialty Food Store sells Italian specialty groceries and prepared foods, operates a restaurant, and offers catering services as well (950 Portage Avenue, www.deluca.ca).

33 Duff Roblin Park
The Red River Floodway story

Although a steel viewing platform catches your eye, Duff Roblin Provincial Park at first appears unremarkable. The platform seems to overlook nothing but a flat landscape and a wide ditch. But that ditch is part of the 47-kilometre (29-mile) Red River Floodway skirting the eastern edge of the city. The Red River runs through Winnipeg and is prone to spring flooding. So, when the floodway gates are activated, some of the river flow is diverted into the floodway and bypasses the city before emptying back into the river. Winnipeggers tend to take that flood protection for granted.

Interpretive panels in the park tell the story of Premier Dufferin Roblin (1917–2010), provincial parks, and the floodway itself, a project championed by Roblin. Opponents dubbed it "Roblin's Folly" and said it would never work. Duff's Ditch, as it was also called, was built between 1962 and 1968. At the time, it was the second largest earth-moving project in the world, second only to the Panama Canal. A bulldozer similar to the ones used to dig the ditch sits in the park.

Built to withstand the kind of flood that comes along once in a hundred years, the floodway did indeed work and has saved the city billions of dollars. It actually reached capacity during the 1997 Flood of the Century. Enhancements completed in 2010 increased its capacity to handle a one-in-700-year flood. The floodway can now divert up to the equivalent of 1.6 Olympic-sized swimming pools of water per second.

The viewing platform overlooks the southern end of the floodway and its Inlet Control Structure, located on a bridge over the Red River. Look through the viewfinder for a closer view. The gates that control the flow of water are beneath the bridge in the Red River. After going through the park displays, you will look at the National Historic Civil Engineering Site from the platform with new eyes and greater appreciation. It no longer appears unremarkable.

Address Courchaine Road, Winnipeg, MB, +1 (204) 945-7273, www.gov.mb.ca/sd/parks, parks@gov.mb.ca | Getting there By car, drive south on St. Mary's Road, turn west onto Courchaine Road or drive south on Highway 75, turn southeast onto Turnbull Drive, turn east onto Courchaine Road | Hours Unrestricted | Tip Walk, run, bike, or ski on the Duff Roblin Parkway Trail, which follows the floodway channel (www.gov.mb.ca/mti/wms/rrf/duffroblin.html).

34 Dugald Grain Elevator
A reminder of a one-time prairie icon

The wooden grain elevator at Dugald stands as one of only a few such structures remaining. Situated alongside railway lines and towering prominently in the flat prairie landscape, these landmarks, sometimes called prairie sentinels or prairie cathedrals, stored grain before it was shipped to worldwide markets. Winnipeg was a major grain centre and a transportation hub in this process. Ogilvie Flour Mills built the Dugald elevator in 1948. It was later owned by Manitoba Pool Elevators and its successor Agricore, who added a wooden crib annex and three steel tanks. It is now privately owned.

The current elevator replaced one that burned in the September 1947 Dugald Train Disaster. On the Monday of the Labour Day weekend, the Minaki Campers Special carrying cottagers returning to the city from Minaki, Ontario collided with the Toronto-bound Transcontinental Special as it paused at the Dugald Station. Gas tanks supplying fuel for the train's lighting exploded and set the mostly wooden passenger cars on fire, killing 31 people. A mass grave in Winnipeg's Brookside cemetery holds 22 of those victims. The funeral cortège was one of the largest in the city's history.

Wooden grain elevators came into use in the 1880s and employed a combination of conveyors, agent-operated levers, and gravity to store grain in bulk, a more efficient process than the previous method of shoveling grain into sacks. They once dotted the prairies, and farmers didn't have far to travel to deliver their grain. The elevators became gathering spots for farmers and an important aspect of the community. But with changes in farming practices and advancements in technology, wooden elevators were replaced by more efficient, large, concrete terminals consolidated in fewer locations.

The Dugald elevator reminds us of both the historical importance of a prairie icon and of that disastrous day in history.

Address Elevator Road, Dugald, MB | **Getting there** By car, drive east on Dugald Road (Highway 15) past Provincial Road 206, turn north on Elevator Road | **Hours** Viewable from the outside only | **Tip** A monument and signage at the eastern edge of the fairgrounds at the Springfield Curling Club entrance commemorates the Dugald Train Disaster (27019 Dugald Road, Dugald).

35 Eddy's Place
Home-cooking and camaraderie in iconic diner

A wrap-around counter, booths with orange acrylic tabletops, and orange-patterned carpet on the upper half of one wall give Eddy's Place the atmosphere from another era. But the welcome you feel when entering the bustling diner is very much of the present. There is no background music, only the hum of friendly banter. Regulars interrupt their conversations to let you know you can take a seat anywhere and will likely offer you menu suggestions. A group of players may be gathered around one of the two snooker tables – some of them store their cues in the restaurant's closet. Although the tables are of a newer vintage, they are a nod to the history of this Selkirk Avenue institution.

Eddy Koranicki took over a combination barbershop/pool hall called Al's in 1955 and renamed it Eddy's sometime in the 1960s. His wife Marie started serving food in 1970. In 1977, three pool tables were removed to make room for booths. Koranicki died in 1992, and Marie sold the restaurant in 1999. It went through several owners until Tanis Desrochers, whom you'll now see cooking at the grill, her partner Daniel Gougeon, and his mother Annette Gougeon bought it in 2012. Annette, now deceased, had been Koranicki's sister-in-law and a long-time cook and server at the restaurant.

When asked about the best menu choices, a regular mentions the burgers and the homemade soups before quickly saying everything is good. Other items on the menu include a large selection of breakfast items, kuby & perogies, salads, wraps, daily specials, and piled-high sandwiches, including the Reuben, corned beef on rye, and two sandwiches named after regulars. Sonny's Sandwich is a burger on thick rye bread. Teddy's Ultimate Ham Sandwich features ham, cheddar, and condiments on thick rye bread.

Eddy's great food will bring a smile to your stomach. Its community feel will bring a smile to your heart.

Address 669 Selkirk Avenue, Winnipeg, MB R2W 2N4, +1 (204) 582-4768 | Getting there Bus 16 to Selkirk & McKenzie (Stops 30276/30277) | Hours Sept–May: Mon–Fri 7am–2pm, Sat 8am–2pm; June–Aug: Mon–Fri 7am–2pm | Tip The Ukrainian Labour Temple was the first and largest labour hall in Canada and has remained a centre of Ukrainian culture for decades. It is a National Historic Site (591 Pritchard Avenue, www.ult-wpg.ca).

36 Elm Park Bridge
The ice cream pedestrian bridge

You may find it hard to believe the narrow Elm Park Bridge, now open only to pedestrians and cyclists, was used for two-way vehicular traffic until 1974. It is sometimes called the BDI Bridge because Bridge Drive-In, a popular ice cream shop commonly referred to as BDI, sits on the north side. A stroll over the bridge and a wander through the Kingston Crescent neighbourhood on the south side, is part of the ice cream ritual for many.

The steel truss bridge, constructed between 1912 and 1913, allowed access to a new residential development in the former Elm Park. Elm Park, which was gradually sold off as individual forest lots starting in 1908, had been a private park located where a bend in the Red River created a small peninsula. People crossed a pontoon bridge to visit the park and its mature elm trees. Those travelling across the new bridge paid a toll to help offset the cost of construction. When the St. Vital municipal government purchased the bridge in 1945, they removed the toll.

Placards on the south side of the bridge tell the story of Elm Park and the residential development. Today's Kingston Crescent neighbourhood is known for its character homes, tree canopy, and large river lots. That tree canopy, however, is not what it was in the days of Elm Park's majestic forest. One of the placards talks about the toll development, disease, and old age has taken and encourages us to care for the trees. Look for the placards beside the giant tree sculpture. The *Dancing Golden Bear* was designed by artist Kevin Kelly and carved by Fred Thomas.

The Bridge Drive-In on the north side has been serving ice cream, sundaes, and shakes since 1957. Some consider its yearly opening the unofficial start of spring. You might want to try the Goog Special, a blueberry upside-down thick shake topped with sliced banana, hot fudge sauce, whipped cream, and a cherry.

Address 766 Jubilee Avenue, Winnipeg, MB R3L 1P8 (north side); Kingston Crescent at Riverdale Avenue (south side) | Getting there Bus BLUE or 47 to Southwest Transitway at Jubilee | Hours Unrestricted | Tip A walk over the Assiniboine Park pedestrian bridge with an ice cream from family-owned Sargent Sundae is another summertime Winnipeg tradition (2053 Portage Avenue, @sargentsundae on Instagram).

37 *Famous Five* Monument
Honouring feminist pioneers and the Persons Case

Until 1929, women were not considered "persons" in Canada. The *Famous Five* monument on the Manitoba Legislative Building grounds celebrates the women who changed the status quo. The bronze sculpture by Helen Granger Young (1922–2023) features five prominent Canadian suffragists at a round table, three standing and two seated: Henrietta Muir Edwards (1849–1931), Emily Murphy (1868–1933), Irene Parlby (1868–1965), Louise McKinney (1868–1931), and Nellie McClung (1873–1951).

In 1927, these women petitioned the Supreme Court for a ruling on the interpretation of the word "persons." The 1867 British North America Act said only qualified persons could be appointed to the Senate. It didn't specifically exclude women, but the government interpreted it that way several times. In 1928, the Court ruled unanimously that women were not "persons," based on what would have been intended in 1867. The women appealed to the Judicial Council of the Privy Council in London, England, Canada's highest court of appeal until 1949. The Privy Council concluded the word did indeed include women. It was a landmark decision.

In the sculpture, the woman seated at the right and signing her name on the petition is Nellie McClung. Born in rural Manitoba, novelist, teacher, and social reformer McClung moved to Winnipeg in 1911 with her husband and four children. An effective speaker, she played a key role in the fight for women to get the vote in her home province. She then moved to Alberta, where she continued her activism a year before that right was finally granted in 1916.

These five women were pioneers of Canadian feminism, and the *Famous Five* monument, unveiled in 2010, recognizes the significance of their contribution to women's rights. They are honoured with two other monuments in Canada, one on Parliament Hill in Ottawa and one in Calgary's Olympic Plaza.

Address 450 Broadway Avenue, Winnipeg, MB R3C 0V8, +1 (204) 945-5813, www.gov.mb.ca/legislature, tour_reservation@leg.gov.mb.ca | Getting there Bus 16, 18, or 60 to Osborne & Broadway (Stops 10596/10599) or bus 10, 17, 20, or 23 to Broadway & Osborne East (Stops 10585/10870) | Hours Unrestricted | Tip A plaque at the former Free Press building honours women's rights activist Cora Hind (1861–1942), an acclaimed Manitoba Free Press agricultural journalist from 1901 to 1942 (300 Carleton Street).

38_Feast Café | Bistro
Modern dishes rooted in Indigenous traditions

You'll feel a warm welcome at Feast Café | Bistro. Indigenous art and framed old photographs adorn the light-filled space. This Indigenous-owned restaurant features a menu of modern dishes rooted in traditional First Nations and Métis cuisine. Bison and bannock figure prominently. Other food staples include pickerel, wild rice, squash, and fresh vegetables. For a sweet and refreshing end to your meal, try the sweetgrass ice cream. All the food here is hand-made from ingredients sourced first from Indigenous and local producers.

Owner and Executive Chef Christa Bruneau-Guenther, a proud member of Peguis First Nation and born and raised in Winnipeg, is a home cook turned restaurateur. Her passion for traditional foods began when developing a healthy food program for day care children, many of whom had ADHD and behavioural problems. Working with Canada's Food Guide for First Nations, Métis, and Inuit People, she learned about traditional foods and grew some in her garden. She spent years studying Indigenous food, learning from elders, and cooking for the community. She says opening the restaurant took a huge leap of faith, and it's fortunate for her customers that she took on that challenge. Her recipes have been featured in national magazines, and she's been a chef judge on *Wall of Chefs* and *Top Chef Canada*.

Bruneau-Guenther describes herself as "community driven, not culinary driven." Mindful of the angels who helped her, she hires staff who might otherwise face employment barriers. They've become a family who greet you with friendly smiles. Feast supports local organizations, feeds soup and bannock to needy community members, and is committed to environmental responsibility.

For Bruneau-Guenther, food is the most powerful thing to connect people with culture and history, providing a sense of pride and self-worth. Feast celebrates that connection with superb dishes.

Address 587 Ellice Avenue, Winnipeg, MB R3B 1Z7, +1 (204) 691-5979, www.feastcafebistro.com, feastcafebistro@gmail.com | Getting there Bus 14 to Ellice & Sherbrook (Stops 10528/10529) | Hours Tue–Sat 11am–10pm (flexible) | Tip The West End Cultural Centre hosts musical concerts in a colourful former church and has won the Western Canadian Music Award for Venue of the Year several times (586 Ellice Avenue, www.wecc.ca).

39 __ Garbage Hill
City views from a former landfill

Westview Park, a hill rising up in the midst of a business and industrial area, comes as a bit of a surprise in a city of flat terrain. Popular with dog walkers and winter tobogganers, the top of the hill provides amazing city views, as Winnipeg's downtown skyline stretches out below you to the East. In the evening, catch sunset views to the West.

A short, narrow road, closed to vehicular traffic in winter, curves up and around the hill at the southern end of the park and leads to a small parking lot. With a wooden railing along a steep drop on one side and the hill forming a wall on the other, this is the closest thing to a mountain drive you'll find in or around Winnipeg. There is also a walking trail to the hilltop, where a compass-shaped monument of concrete blocks provides a good spot from which to take in the views as does the trail along the hill perimeter.

Nature did not create this hill. Rather, the Saskatchewan Avenue landfill was converted into a park in 1960 and officially named Westview Park. But Winnipeggers refer to it as Garbage Hill. A Hollywood-style sign on the east side overlooks the road and spells out "Garbage Hill" in large, white letters. The city erected the sign in 2018 in response to public outcry after they'd dismantled an unapproved sign of scrap wood erected by an unnamed artist.

As per a February 16, 1961 *Winnipeg Free Press* article, one of the rejected names for the park was Ginger Snooks' Paradise. Garbage collector Albert Roger "Ginger" Snook (1835–1926) had been a colourful character who lost frequent runs for city council and livened up meetings with his outbursts and antics. Alderman William McGarva suggested the name Westview Park because of the good view to the West, although Parks Board member J. J. Thomas argued the view was equally good on the other side. You'll likely agree with Thomas.

Address 1 Midland Street, Winnipeg, MB R3E 3J6, parkmaps.winnipeg.ca | Getting there Bus 20 to Wellington & Empress (Stops 10388/10397) or bus 15 to Sargent & Sanford (Stops 10453/10454) | Hours Daily 7am – 10pm | Tip For a nostalgic and sophisticated dinner, visit Rae & Jerry's Steakhouse, where a retro interior and a classic steak house menu take you back in time (1405 Portage Avenue, www.raeandjerrys.com).

40 Geological Sciences Museum

There's fossils in them there buildings

Tyndall Stone, a mottled, cream-coloured, dolomitic limestone, is associated with Manitoba architecture. The presence of fossils creates the stone's distinctive mottling. You'll find it in Winnipeg buildings of varying styles and ages, from the Manitoba Legislative Building, to the Centennial Concert Hall, to the Canadian Museum for Human Rights. In 2022, the International Commission on Geoheritage recognized Tyndall Stone as one of 32 heritage stones world-wide – it's the only Canadian stone on the list.

Used as a building material for nearly 200 years, the stone became known as Tyndall in the early twentieth century. Tyndall was the name of the nearest railway station to Garson, where the stone is quarried, and the name is now trademarked by Gillis Quarries Ltd. The University of Manitoba's Geological Sciences Museum tells the whole story.

A Wallace Building hallway hosts the R. B. Ferguson Museum of Mineralogy exhibits. Walk on to reach the Ed Leith Cretaceous Menagerie, where four skeletal replicas of creatures from millions of years ago create a dramatic entrance. An aggressive tyrannosaurid dinosaur looks ready to attack. Three sea monsters hang suspended from the ceilings. Panels describe the Cretaceous Period and Cretaceous rocks and fossils of Manitoba. The adjacent rows of display cases contain Geological Sciences Museum exhibits of fossils, minerals, rocks, and a seismograph.

Look for a Tyndall Stone sample among coral rocks in the front row display case. The "Ancient Marine Life in Tyndall Exhibit" along the back row provides more information and shows you how to identify the organisms that lived in Manitoba's Ordovician-age sea 450 million years ago by the fossil shapes and designs found in the stone. Once you exit, notice Tyndall stone on the building itself.

Address 125 Dysart Road, Winnipeg, MB R3T 2N2, +1 (204) 474-9371, www.umanitoba.ca/environment-earth-resources | Getting there Bus Blue, 47, 60, 74, 75, 78, 662, 671, or 672 to U of M | Hours Mon – Fri 8:30am – 4:30pm (except University holidays) | Tip St. Andrews on the Red Anglican Church, the oldest surviving stone church in Western Canada and a National Historic Site, is a notable early Tyndall-stone structure (St. Andrews, MB, www.standrewsonthered.ca).

41 — Granite Curling Club

You're welcome at Winnipeg's oldest curling club

A brick and half-timbered building with two large gables and dormer windows appears to be a Tudor cottage. But it is actually the club-house for the Granite Curling Club, the oldest such institution in Winnipeg. Their Saturday Learn to Curl "Drop-In" program introduces new players to one of the world's oldest team sports, dating back to the 1600s.

Scottish settlers brought curling to Manitoba in the late 1800s. Initially played on frozen rivers, the sport moved to public skating rinks and then indoor curling rinks. The game involves two teams of four players, each taking turns to slide granite stones toward a target known as the "house." Curling is a popular winter pastime in Winnipeg, which is home to the Manitoba Open Bonspiel, the largest curling tournament in the world.

The Learn to Curl league runs almost every Saturday during curling season, introducing new players to the game and refreshing those who haven't curled in a while. Volunteers provide beginner, intermediate, and experienced instruction levels. Teams are then formed to play short, fun games. The league operates on a drop-in basis, so you can show up once to try the game and come back to hone your skill.

The Granite Curling Club, formed in 1880, first played on sheets of ice beneath a tent. In 1892, they built their own indoor rink. They purchased the land at their current location along the Assiniboine River in 1911, and they were the first Winnipeg curling club to install artificial ice in 1953. Over the years, they have produced several championship curlers. What a perfect place to learn the sport sometimes referred to as "the roaring game" because of the roar of the noise made as a granite stone travels over the ice.

In summer months, the parking lot of the curling club becomes home to The Beer Can, an outdoor beer garden offering food and a large selection of Manitoba craft beers.

Address 1 Granite Way, Winnipeg, MB R3C 0Y9, +1 (204) 775-8239, www.granitecurlingclub.ca, curl@granitecurlingclub.ca | Getting there Bus 16, 18, or 60 to Osborne & Granite (Stop 10600) or Osborne & Assiniboine (Stop 10595) | Hours See website for schedule | Tip The south face of the St. Vital Curling Club features a mural honouring the Jennifer Jones curling team, who won a gold medal at the 2014 Winter Olympics in Sochi (286 Regal Avenue, www.stvitalcurling.ca).

42 Happyland Park
Winnipeg's first permanent disc golf course

If you aren't familiar with disc golf, you may wonder why the south end of Happyland Park has metal poles supporting odd-looking baskets made of metal chains. These are the "holes" in the game of disc golf. Instead of knocking a golf ball into a hole in the ground with a club, you toss a disc – similar to a Frisbee but smaller, heavier, and more aerodynamic – into a basket on a pole. The object of the game is to land the disc into the basket in the fewest throws possible. The course at Happyland Park opened in 2001 and was Winnipeg's first permanent disc golf course.

Disc golf players begin each hole by throwing their disc from the designated "Tee Pad" area. Concrete pads at Happyland mark the tee. If the disc doesn't land in the basket, you make your next throw from the spot where it landed. Similar to counting shots in regular golf, you count the number of throws it took to get the disc into the basket. Low score wins the game. Anyone can play disc golf. You don't need any expensive gear. There are no dress codes and no green fees. All you need is a disc and a scorecard.

Discs come in a variety of sizes and weights. More experienced players may wish to experiment with different discs for varying distances from the basket, but you only need one disc to start playing the game. Use whatever throwing style you feel comfortable with. Disc golf can be played year-round, but you may have to adjust your throwing technique in winter to account for extra layers of clothing that limit range of motion, not to mention the cold air causing discs to stiffen.

No reservations are required to play a round of 9 or 18 holes at Happyland Park. Group size is limited to five people, and the etiquette rules are posted. Some of the rules are the same as in regular golf, such as allowing faster groups to play through and yelling "Fore" if a disc is heading for someone on the course.

Address 520 Marion Street, Winnipeg MB, parkmaps.winnipeg.ca | Getting there Bus 19 to Marion & Dufresne (Stops 50260/50261); course is at south end of park bordering Prosper Street | Hours Unrestricted | Tip If miniature golf is more your style, head to The Golf Dome's indoor 18-hole miniature golf course for fun and challenging putting year-round (1205 Wilkes Avenue, www.thegolfdome.ca).

43 Hell's Alley

Remembering terror on Elgin Avenue

An alley off Main Street became known as Hell's Alley after the violent events of Bloody Saturday during the 1919 Winnipeg General Strike. The Centennial Concert Hall now stands where the alley would have connected to Main Street, but a block to the east you can get a sense of what being in that alley on that day must have felt between brick warehouse walls and buildings with metal fire escapes that line the sides of narrow Elgin Avenue. You can still see loading dock numbers in the brick on some buildings. Remnants of railway tracks remain embedded in the street, as a spur railway line ran along the alley at one time to transport goods directly from warehouses to the main transfer railway.

The 1919 Winnipeg General Strike, a major event in the history of the province and Canada, began on May 15, 1919. Over 30,000 workers walked off their jobs and shut down the city for six weeks. On Saturday, June 21, when the strike was in its sixth week, tens of thousands of strike supporters gathered in front of City Hall to protest the arrests of several strike leaders. When a streetcar driven by strikebreakers came down the street, demonstrators rocked it off its tracks and later set the empty car on fire. Northwest Mounted Police and untrained special constables, armed with clubs and guns, rode into the crowd. Fighting spilled into the alley, and the 10-minute conflict led to 27 casualties.

Standing in the middle of this block of Elgin Avenue today, you can easily imagine the terror people must have felt as they fled the violence on Main Street only to become trapped in the confines of the alley. The Bloody Saturday confrontation resulted in two deaths and dozens of injuries. The strike ended four days later. Although the workers received no improvement to wages or working conditions, the strike is considered an influential milestone in the trajectory of Canada's labour movement.

Address Elgin Avenue between Lily and Bertha Streets, Winnipeg, MB | Getting there Bus 11, 15, 16, 18, 20, 21, 24, 44, 45, or 47 to Main & James (Stops 10629/10634) | Hours Unrestricted | Tip The leaning, sinking streetcar sculpture *Bloody Saturday* by Bernie Miller and Noam Gonick commemorates the 1919 General Strike (Pantages Plaza at Main Street & Market Avenue, www.winnipegarts.ca/public-art).

44 Henteleff Park

A riverside park with a rich history

Although surrounded by development, Henteleff Park in south Winnipeg retains its rural character. Nestled along the eastern edge of the Red River, the 16.9-hectare (42-acre) park is a natural urban oasis with a diversity of plants and wildlife. You'll find forest, grassland, and riverbank, as well as all 16 of Manitoba's native deciduous tree species. Over 150 species of songbirds nest and use the park during their migration. Normand Creek, a seasonal tributary in the park, floods every spring to create a backwater resting, feeding, and spawning area for more than 10 species of fish. Follow the park's wood chip trails for a peaceful nature walk.

The Métis people had settled along the Red and Assiniboine Rivers in long narrow strips of land known as river lots. This settlement pattern gave each family access to the river and strengthened ties among neighbours. The park was such a lot when the Henteleff family, for whom the park is named, purchased it in the early 1920s. They became one of Winnipeg's first Jewish market gardeners. Son Nathan Henteleff inherited the land in 1934. He was known as the "Cabbage King of Manitoba" and was famous for his pickles. The city expropriated the land in 1967 for a park, but wound up using it as a tree nursery. Efforts by Friends of Henteleff Park, founded in 1996, resulted in the area being designated as Henteleff Park in 2002. Today, you'll find native vegetation and riparian forest as well as rows of ornamental trees. Interpretive panels at the entrance provide details about the landscape, the park's Métis and market gardening roots, and the Henteleff family.

Maintained by the volunteer-run Henteleff Park Foundation, which continues to restore the natural areas, the park provides a respite from the busy city, a chance to get closer to nature, and a place for quiet reflection. Enjoy a stress-reducing nature stroll year-round, as the park's walking trails are beautiful in all seasons.

Address 1964 St. Mary's Road, Winnipeg, MB R2N 4G8, www.henteleffpark.org | Getting there Bus 14 to St. Mary's & Warde (Stops 50192/50685) | Hours Unrestricted | Tip Find everything to feed wild birds in your own yard as well as nature-related gift items, garden décor, and crystals at The Preferred Perch (4-1604 St. Mary's Road, www.thepreferredperch.ca).

45 Historic Hamilton House
Gag gifts and paranormal activity

Gags Unlimited sells balloons, silly gifts, novelty items, and costumes from the main floor of a house known for its history of paranormal research, psychic experiments, and haunted phenomena. Given that history, it seems fitting today's Historic Hamilton House offers psychic readings, metaphysical events, and ghost hunting equipment in addition to party supplies.

From 1910 until his death in 1935, Dr. T. G. Hamilton ran his medical practice from the main floor and basement of the house while his family lived in the upper two floors. After Dr. Hamilton's three-year-old son died of the Spanish flu in 1919, he began to investigate spiritual communication with the deceased. The séances he conducted as part of his scientific research became world-famous, attracting visitors such as Prime Minister William Lyon Mackenzie King and Sir Arthur Conan Doyle, creator of *Sherlock Holmes*. Hamilton and his wife Lillian meticulously documented and photographed his psychic experiments. He recorded instances of table tipping, ectoplasm, trance states, and automatic writing. His papers are now stored in the University of Manitoba Archives. Cheryl Wiebe of Gags Unlimited bought the house in 2021.

Historic Hamilton House's website says an important aspect of sharing the house with the public is to honour its history, rebuild its energies, and learn from it. Mediums conduct psychic readings in the room where Dr. Hamilton once held séances. Special events include metaphysical workshops, astrology birthday events, and group séances, and you can take a house tour to learn more about Dr. Hamilton, the house, and lingering spirits. People have heard furniture moving in rooms with no one in them. A photojournalist had batteries on many of his electronics die when shooting interviews in the house. Keep your wits about you in case you too sense a strong paranormal presence when you visit!

Address 185 Henderson Highway, Winnipeg, MB R2L 1L5, +1 (204) 453-0133, www.historichamiltonhouse.ca, enquiries@gagsunlimited.com | Getting there Bus 11 to Henderson & Gordon (Stop 40369) or Henderson & Hespeler (Stop 40437) | Hours Store: Mon–Wed & Sat 10am–5pm, Thu & Fri 10am–6pm; see website for events | Tip The ghost of Joseph Norman MacDonald, who died in 1912 at age three, is said to play in Elmwood Cemetery, where the Hamiltons are buried (88 Hespeler Avenue, www.historicelmwoodcemetery.ca).

46 Humboldt's Legacy

Where you can feel extra good about shopping

It's a delight to browse the shelves at Humboldt's Legacy. You'll feel good browsing through the shop's attractive displays and its wide variety of lovely products. You can also feel good when you make a purchase because the items are sustainable and fair trade. The store, which describes itself as "Winnipeg's Good Conscience Store" on its Instagram page, offers something for everyone.

Owners Kris and Will Kurtz opened one of North America's oldest sustainable, economy, neighbourhood stores in 1989 as a way of doing their part to make the world a better place. They offered consumers a chance to vote with their dollars. It was the first store in Winnipeg to sell recycled paper and biodegradable cleaning products. Humboldt's Legacy has grown from the initial tiny shop, which stocked only a few products, into a mini department store. Regular customers come from all over the city.

Products include eco-friendly toys, healthy beauty products, baby shampoos, biodegradable household cleaners, and kitchen accessories. You'll find fashionable men's and women's clothing in organic fabrics and bamboo, gloves and mitts, socks, babywear, colourful children's sweaters, hats, scarves, and bamboo underwear. Home décor items include candles, Turkish sheets, blankets, porcelain tableware, and more. Don't miss the fair-trade chocolate and gourmet food items. In a freezer at the back, you'll even find grass-fed meat from a small farmer and fish caught in clean, cold, northern lake waters. And get a giggle or two from the greeting card collection.

When Kris Kurtz thinks about the decisions she makes about which products to stock, she says, "Sometimes I think I should rename the store Stuff I Like." You're sure to find plenty of stuff you like too. Whether you're looking for something for yourself or hunting for a gift, the shopping experience at Humboldt's Legacy is always fun.

Address 167 Lilac Street, Winnipeg, MB R3M 2S1, +1 (204) 772-1404, www.humboldtslegacy.com, info@humboldtslegacy.com | Getting there Bus 18 to Corydon & Lilac (Stops 10130/10140) | Hours Mon–Sat 10am–6pm, Sun noon–5pm | Tip Bring your own containers to Planet Pantry in the Johnston Terminal at The Forks to fill up on ethically sourced soaps, cleaners, and bath and beauty products (25 Forks Market Road, www.planetpantry.ca).

47   ideaMILL

Your gateway to creativity and community

At the ideaMILL makerspace in Winnipeg's downtown Millennium Library, you can explore your creative side, learn new skills, and bring your ideas to life with free access to a variety of tools and technologies. All you need is a library card.

Learn to sew or complete a sewing project at one of several sewing machines. There's also a serger, an embroidery machine, a quilting sewing machine, and an industrial sewing machine. Digitize old photos, videos, cassettes, or records. Create your own custom greeting card, vinyl decal, or personalized t-shirt with the Cricut cutter and heat press. Book the DSLR camera, photobox, or backdrop and lighting kit to do your own photo shoot or film a family video. Create your own podcast, demo, or audiobook in one of the two sound booths. If you need an instrument, an acoustic guitar and ukuleles are available.

The digital printers are the most popular pieces of equipment. Build your own gaming pieces, fidget spinners, or other items. Imprint your own designs on button badges. Other equipment includes a foam cutter, a Mayku Formbox, and electronics tools, including soldering irons. High-end computers have software to help with your design projects.

Equipment is free to use, but you should book in advance via website or phone. Children under 13 are welcome with a parent or guardian. The ideaMILL stocks a few basic supplies, which you can buy at cost, and staff is on-site to provide basic guidance. In addition to the main maker space, there is a classroom with a smart screen, and a craft room where you can tackle messier projects.

IdeaMILL offers a number of craft workshops and hosts regular sessions for people with shared interests, such as knitting and sewing circles, as well as acoustic music jam sessions. Be prepared to collaborate and share ideas with others while you're here – it's part of the makerspace experience.

Address 251 Donald Street, Winnipeg, MB R3C 3P5, +1 (204) 986-5543, wpl.winnipeg.ca/library/ideamill, ideamill@winnipeg.ca | Getting there Bus BLUE, 16, 17, 18, 20, 33, 44, 45, or 60 to Graham & Donald (Stop 10614) or Graham & Smith (Stop 10615) or bus 10, 11, 14, 15, 19, 21, 24, 38, 43, or 55 to Portage & Donald (Stops 10542/10582) | Hours See website for hours and events | Tip Just outside, Millennium Library Park is an urban oasis with prairie and parkland grasses, a wetland, rest areas, and public art installations (251 Donald Street).

48 — Into The Music

Best vinyl in the prairies

You'll find almost every music genre you can imagine at Into the Music – and there's a lot to look through. Located on the first floor of a historic building in the Exchange District, this shop sells used and new vinyl records and CDs, rare music DVDs, books, and magazines, as well as posters and t-shirts. The large space features tall windows, high ceilings, an old wood floor, and row upon row of bins containing records and CDs grouped by genre. Clearly and artfully labelled, the rows invite you to browse. The space encourages you to explore nooks and crannies for treasures and to have a chat with staff and other shoppers. A welcoming atmosphere entices you to linger.

The store's selection includes more than 20,000 long-play vinyl records, around 8,000 7-inch records, and 10,000 to 12,000 CDs. And they're all curated. Owner Greg Tonn says he and his staff, all music lovers, know their customers, and they select what they buy from locals and estates based on what their customers want. They clean items up to ensure the best quality sound and label them accordingly. There is a listening station should you want to hear a record before you purchase it.

Tonn first opened the store in 1987. After moving a few times, it has been in its current location since 2003. Demand for records declined in the 1990s, but a revival of vinyl music started in the late 2000s and has brought increased demand and a younger demographic into the store. You can also still find the "oldie" records though.

Bins near the front of the store contain records that are "New This Week." They are refilled each Monday, so on Monday mornings, people line up outside the store at opening time to be the first to see what's in those bins. Whatever day you visit, you'll find a strong sense of community. Join your kindred spirits for live music of varying genres on most Friday evenings.

Address B–245 McDermot Avenue, Winnipeg, MB R3B 0S6, +1 (204) 287-8279, www.intothemusic.ca, info@intothemusic.ca | Getting there Bus 11, 15, 16, 18, 20, 21, 24, 44, 45, or 47 to Main & McDermot (Stops 10628/10636) or Main & Lombard (Stop 10637) | Hours Mon–Thu & Sat 10:30am–6pm, Fri 10:30am–9pm, Sun 11am–5pm | Tip Visit the two blocks and associated alleys of nearby Albert Street to see murals and graffiti art on sides of buildings.

49 Jai Pereira Memorial

Winnipeg skateboarding community pioneer

At the Plaza at The Forks, Canada's largest urban skate plaza and bowl facility, you'll find a memorial to Winnipeg skateboarding icon, Jai Pereira. Sponsored by Graffiti Art Programming, the mural was painted by internationally renowned, London-based, professional graffiti artist Mr Cenz (Julian Phethean) in 2018, who chose to focus on Pereira's face in striking blue and purple tones. Anyone familiar with Mr Cenz' work will recognize his vibrant, abstract, free form, layered, and futuristic style. But there is something unusual about this piece: Mr Cenz usually paints women, not men. He painted Pereira because of the importance of his story.

Jai Pereira is credited with creating Winnipeg's skateboarding scene. As owner of Sk8 Skates, one of the longest standing skateboard shops in Canada, he brought professional skateboarders to Winnipeg for demonstrations, ran local competitions, organized community events, sponsored local skateboarders, and advocated for skateboarding. Sk8 Skates became a hub for Winnipeg skateboarders, as Pereira created a welcoming community for everyone, including kids on the outskirts of society. In addition to promoting skateboarding, he also supported local bands. Pat Lazo of Graffiti Art Programming described Pereira as "a 'rooting for the underdog' kind of guy." Pereira and his partner Alana Lowry were killed in a motorcycling accident in 2001. Pereira was 34.

The Plaza at The Forks, which opened in 2006, is considered one of the best skateboard parks in Canada. The world-class facility has attracted world-famous skateboard pros and is used regularly by BMX cyclists as well as skateboarders. Although Pereira did not live to see this park, it seems a fitting place for a mural to honour his memory and the impact he made. Look beside the skatepark and behind the Winnipeg sign for the mural. Its fluorescent colours glow at night.

Address Israel Asper Way at The Forks, Winnipeg, MB, www.theforks.com, info@theforks.com | **Getting there** Bus 38 to Israel Asper & Canadian Museum for Human Rights (Stops 10901/10902) | **Hours** Unrestricted | **Tip** A Mr Cenz mural on the side of the Indigenous Family Centre (470 Selkirk Avenue) in memory of missing and murdered Indigenous women and girls shows the face of a young Indigenous woman.

50 James Avenue Pumphouse

Historic pumphouse turned trendy restaurant

In front of James Avenue Pumphouse Food & Drink, an old fire hose cart and weathered fire hydrants bookmarking a bicycle rack hint at what the historic building used to be. Inside this former water pumping station, a friendly space with a mix of high and low tables welcomes you. Brick walls, large windows, and wood tables create warmth, while exposed pipework and a high ceiling bring a modern, industrial vibe. Firefighter helmets hang on the wall. The top shelf behind the bar displays antique fire extinguishers. Floor-to-ceiling windows at one end provide a captivating view of the vintage pumping machinery.

In 1904, a serious fire forced the city to pump Assiniboine River water into the mains, thereby contaminating the water supply and causing a typhoid epidemic. So, the James Avenue Pumping Station was built in 1906 to create a better water supply system for firefighting. A high-pressure system, one of the largest and most sophisticated in the world at the time, drew water from the nearby Red River and distributed it to downtown hydrants. The coal-powered pumps were converted to natural gas and electricity in 1962. The facility, designated a municipal heritage site in 1982, closed in 1986. Although projects to revive the building were discussed, it sat empty for decades. James Avenue Pumphouse Food & Drink, part of a larger development project, opened in fall 2021.

Drawing on Manitoba's culinary traditions and global comfort food inspirations, the menu here offers something for everyone, including vegan, vegetarian, and gluten-sensitive options. The drinks menu features a good selection of craft beer, wine, and spirits, as well as classic cocktails and trademark drinks with fun names evoking tunes from the 1990s and 2000s, like "Nothing But a Tea Thang" and "Tropic Like It's Hot." Come here for food, drinks, and an enjoyable time out with family or friends.

Address 2-109 James Avenue, Winnipeg, MB R3B 0N6, +1 (204) 560-5210, www.jamesavenuepumphouse.com, office@jamespumphouse.ca | Getting there Bus 11, 15, 16, 18, 20, 21, 24, 44, 45, or 47 to Main & James (Stops 10629/10634) | Hours Mon–Thu 11am–11pm, Fri & Sat 11am–midnight, Sun 11am–10pm | Tip The Winnipeg Fire-fighters Museum, located in a former firehall, shares antique vehicles, fire-fighting apparatus, and memorabilia across two floors (56 Maple Street, www.wpgfiremuseum.ca).

51 Jane's
Fine dining in a classroom

Located in Western Canada's oldest skyscraper, Jane's offers fine dining while also providing training to Culinary Arts and Hospitality Management students. Construction on the Union Bank building, now Red River College Polytechnic's Paterson GlobalFoods Institute, was finished in 1904, and its former banking hall now houses the restaurant. The opulent room features a marble floor, large arched windows, ornate coffered ceilings, and marble columns.

Open for several weeks during fall and winter terms, Jane's serves lunch and dinner on Tuesdays through Fridays. First-year students cycle through lunch shifts, and second-year students work at dinner time. Culinary students prepare the food – you can view the busy, white-hatted chefs in the open-concept kitchen. Hospitality students bring the plates to your table. Second-year culinary students also take on serving shifts to give them broader experience. All the while, instructors guide, observe, and grade their students' performance.

Instructors develop the menus to include diverse foods and a variety of techniques with soups, salads, mains, and desserts. The lunch menu has a Canadian regional focus and stays the same for the term. The dinner menu, which also includes appetizers, changes about every three weeks. Culinary students prepare a lunch-time special as part of the curriculum. Mixology students create a dinner cocktail.

With elegant surroundings, fine cuisine artfully displayed on the plate, and attentive service, there is nothing "plain Jane" about dining at Jane's. You can enjoy upscale dining and have the satisfaction of knowing you are helping students develop skills through real-life experience. For a less formal meal, visit the Culinary Exchange food court, another college restaurant in the same building. Open weekdays year-round, it offers breakfast and lunch items prepared by culinary students.

Address 504 Main Street, Winnipeg, MB R3B 0T1, +1 (204) 632-2594, www.rrc.ca/janes, janes@rrc.ca | Getting there Bus 11, 15, 16, 18, 20, 21, 24, 44, 45, or 47 to Main & McDermot (Stops 10628/10636) or Main & Lombard (Stop 10637) | Hours See website | Tip See the plaque on the north side of the same building honouring the International Brotherhood of Magicians, which was founded in 1922 on the 7th floor and would become the world's largest body of magicians.

52 Jewish Heritage Centre
Remembering and educating

You'll want to take your time in the Elaine and Percy Goldberg Family Walkway at the Asper Jewish Community Campus. Windows along one wall provide views into a large display case featuring exhibits of the Marion and Ed Vickar Jewish Museum of Western Canada. Changing exhibitions, which can run for several years, showcase Western Canadian Jewish history and culture. Exhibitions have covered such topics as Jewish farm settlements, the garment industry, Jewish contributions to local theatre, history of the YMHA, and the contributions made by Jewish women. Items in the photographic gallery on the opposite wall relate to the current display case exhibition or highlight other themes, such as the works of architect Max Blankenstein.

Boxcar-like doors at the end of the display case open into the Freeman Family Holocaust Education Centre. The doors will remind you of the boxcars that took so many people to the death camps during World War II. Inside the room are text panels outlining Holocaust history. Names of survivors who settled in Winnipeg and artifacts donated by Manitoban survivors personalize the factual information. Photographs, diary pages, ghetto tokens, the star "badges" Jews had to wear on their clothing, and swastika-engraved cutlery, along with their associated stories, powerfully convey the Holocaust's impact, alongside a section about life before the Holocaust. An interactive table provides even more information and photographs. Click the video link to access over 56,000 testimonies in the USC Shoah Foundation Visual History Archive.

The Museum and Holocaust Education Centre are part of the Jewish Heritage Centre of Western Canada, which collects and preserves records and traditions of the Jewish community. It has over 4,000 artifacts, 70,000 photographs, 1,300 recordings, 1,000 boxes of records, and 200 bound volumes of newspapers.

Address 123 Doncaster Street, Winnipeg, MB R3N 2B2, +1 (204) 477-7460, www.jhcwc.org, jewishheritage@jhcwc.org | Getting there Bus 66, 74, 78, or 79 to Kenaston & Willow (Stops 60444/60445) | Hours Mon–Thu 6am–9pm, Fri 6am–7pm, Sat & Sun 8am–6pm | Tip Head to family-owned Bernstein's Deli for latkes, corned beef hash, freshly made soups, and all your favorite deli comfort foods (1-1700 Corydon Avenue, www.bernsteinsdeli.com).

53 Kelly House Pillars

Urban legend of pilfered pillars

Upon the front landing of a downtown high-rise apartment building, seven limestone pillars seem to belong to another era. And, indeed, they do. The Kelly House Apartments pillars are all that remain of an elegant mansion that once stood on the same spot. For decades, people believed that the pillars had been stolen from the Manitoba Legislative Building construction project.

The original, private, three-storey house belonged to Thomas Kelly (1855–1939), a Winnipeg contractor. A 1916 postcard in the digitized history collection of PastForward, a Winnipeg Public Library project, features a photograph of the house with the caption, "One of Winnipeg's finest residences." In 1913, the provincial government contracted Kelly's company to construct the new Legislative Building, and costs quickly ballooned. Working with members of the administration of then-Premier Rodmond Roblin (1853–1937), Kelly inflated invoices, substituted cheaper materials, lied about quantities of materials, and funneled some of the proceeds to the ruling Conservative Party's election fund. The fraud came to light and led to the fall of Roblin's government. Kelly was sentenced to two and a half years in prison but served only nine months due to ill health. He moved to Kansas, Missouri, and then California. The province seized his mansion, and it served a variety of purposes before being demolished in 1965.

Given Kelly's massive fraud, it isn't difficult to believe the Kelly House pillars were pilfered from the Legislative Building project. The story was accepted as truth for years – until CBC News debunked the story in 2018. The house was built in 1909 and the pillars appear to have been in place before the Legislative Building contract was awarded. In the end, the story turned out to be an urban myth, but the pillars still remind us of one of Manitoba's biggest scandals.

Address 15 Carlton Street, Winnipeg, MB R3C 1N8 | **Getting there** Bus 23 to Broadway & Carlton (Stop 10592) or Broadway & Edmonton (Stop 10586), or bus 16, 18, or 60 to Osborne & Broadway (Stops 10596/10599) or bus 44 to Carleton & Assiniboine (Stop 10686) | **Hours** Viewable from the outside only | **Tip** Dalnavert Museum is set in the 1895 mansion of Hugh John Macdonald (1850–1929), one-time Premier of Manitoba, and tells the story of the Macdonald family. It is a National Historic Site (61 Carlton Street, www.friendsofdalnavert.ca).

54 Kindness Rock Garden

Happy Tree Rock Garden and Yellow Brick Road

Nancy-Tina Coutu's Happy Tree Kindness Garden sits at the base of a tree between the sidewalk and the street. Resting on a bed of solid-coloured stones inside a rim of green bricks, decorated rocks are adorned with cartoon figures, lady bugs, happy faces, and inspirational sayings. A path of yellow cement blocks leads to the garden and circles it. A basket holds markers for writing messages on the blocks. In the winter, when the garden is covered with tarp and snow, Coutu leaves out a decorated box of kindness rocks.

Before creating the garden, Coutu, as part of the Winnipeg Rocks group, decorated rocks and left them in public places to bring smiles to everyone who found them. In March 2020, when the COVID-19 pandemic shuttered businesses and sent people home, Coutu strung solar-powered fairy lights and hung emoji balls from her tree to bring a bit of joy to her neighbours. She created encouraging messages for essential workers. People dubbed it "The Happy Tree."

So Coutu decided that her happy tree would be a good spot for a kindness garden. Through the Winnipeg Rocks Facebook page, she invited people to come to her garden on July 1 and bring a rock to exchange. Visitors were then inspired to create their own gardens. Coutu now administers a Facebook group for Winnipeg Kindness Rock Gardens and maintains a map of locations for approximately 100 gardens. She says the gardens show amazing creativity and reflect the personality of the creator. Many are family projects.

These gardens promote love and kindness. There are no fees to visit. Rocks are free, but please take only one and leave the rest for others to enjoy. Bring your own decorated rock to "sow" in the garden. Coutu's favourites are those painted by children. Although it's not required, adding your own rock may *be the reason someone smiles*, as the sign at Happy Tree Kindness Garden states.

Address 1402 Leila Avenue, Winnipeg, MB R2P 1J8, www.facebook.com/groups/
876544106478510, omygoshattitude@gmail.com | Getting there Bus 17 or
77 to Leila & Pipeline (Stops 30896/30897) or bus 17 or 33 to Manila & Cartwright
(Stops 30904/30909) | Hours Unrestricted | Tip If you are interested in a different kind of
rock, you can find crystals, geodes, polished stones, and gemstone jewelry at Jacobs Trading
(11–1600 Regent Avenue W, www.jacobstrading.ca).

55 Kudlowich Homestead
Remnants of a former community

Birds Hill Provincial Park is a favourite spot for outdoor activities, but many people may not be aware of a historical site in the park. Kudlowich Homestead was once part of Pine Ridge, a thriving, self-sufficient community created by Polish and Ukrainian immigrants in 1936. Frank and Rose Kudlowich lived on the homestead for seven years. After that, the property became home to Frank's brother's family for another seven years.

You'll find the weathered buildings of the old homestead on a shaded lot on Pine Ridge Trail, a short walk from the trail's parking lot. The family lived on the main floor of the two-storey, hand-constructed log house and used the upper level for storage. The barn housed animals and stored hay. A small granary, built using lumber from an old railway car, served as a summer kitchen as well as grain storage. Placards and signage provide details about homestead life.

A 1920s' Case Company threshing machine sits at the edge of the yard, hinting at the work required to thrive as homesteaders. During the summer months, interpreters are on site at select times to provide insights and stories and allow you to explore the house's interior. Although the furnishings are not original from the Kudlowich family, the pieces on display have been collected from the community to recreate the time period when the family lived here. Look for a Viceroy wood stove, old china cabinets, a radio set, and a working Cecilian gramophone.

Homes were expropriated in the early 1960s to make way for the park. The Pine Ridge Trail is dedicated to the former residents of Pine Ridge and follows what was once Old School Road. The Pine Ridge Trail guide identifies other former community sites in the community and provides information about the residents. Kudlowich Homestead stands as a reminder of what was once a strong independent community of hard-working people.

Address South Drive at Pine Ridge Trail, Birds Hill Park, MB, +1 (204) 654-6730, www.gov.mb.ca/sd/parks/education-and-interpretation/event-listings.html, parks@gov.mb.ca | **Getting there** By car, drive north on Highway 59 24 kilometres to park entrance, and follow South Drive to Pine Ridge Trail | **Hours** Unrestricted from the outside; see website Education and Interpretation events for tour times | **Tip** The Village at Pineridge Hollow contains unique shops, eateries, trails, and a weekend farmers' market (67086 Heatherdale Road, Oakbank, www.pineridgehollow.com).

56 La Maison Gabrielle-Roy
The novelist's beloved home

Now a house museum and National Historic Site, La Maison Gabrielle-Roy was once the home of celebrated French-Canadian novelist Gabrielle Roy. Known for writing on the human condition with a simple style and skillful depictions of everyday life, Roy lived here from her birth in 1909 until 1937. After traveling in Europe, she settled in Québec but remained attached to the house until her death in 1983. The house provided inspiration for many of her works and appears in several of her novels.

From the sidewalk, the yellow, wooden, 1905 house with a wraparound veranda looks warm and welcoming. It is easy to understand Roy's fondness for it. You can view the exterior and grounds year-round, and there are two plaques with information about Roy and the house.

During the summer, visitors can visit the comfortable interior, which has been restored to the time when Roy lived here. Descriptions from her books were used to help with the restoration. Original wood floors remain. Wall colours match those used by the family. Period furnishings include a cast-iron stove, a Singer sewing machine, a round, lace-covered dining table, and a Bell piano with family photos upon it. Two bedrooms on the second level give you insights around the Roy family and Gabrielle's life. Family artifacts include letters, a quilt, a school medal, and a first edition of *Rue Deschambault*. In the third floor/attic you'll find Roy's typewriter. As an adolescent, she took over a room in the attic with a window onto the front street and began writing in that spot.

Roy's first novel was published in 1945. *Bonheur d'Occasion*, or *The Tin Flute*, brought her immediate recognition. She went on to write many more novels and short stories, and she received numerous honours, including three Governor-General awards. Her books, which were originally written in French, were translated into English, as well as many other languages.

Address 375 Deschambault Street, Winnipeg, MB R2H 3B4, +1 (204) 231-3853, www.maisongabrielleroy.mb.ca, info@maisongabrielleroy.mb.ca | Getting there Bus 10 to Des Meurons & Deschambault (Stops 50243/50244) | Hours July & Aug Tue–Sat 10am–4pm | Tip Enjoy craft beer and gourmet hot dogs in the welcoming, retro vibe of Kilter Brewing (450 Deschambault Street, www.kilterbrewing.co).

57 La Parfumerie
Custom blended, natural perfumes

In La Parfumerie, located on the main floor of a three-storey character home, you'll find an attractive display of natural perfumes available for purchase in vials, mists, and hand-crafted bottles and pendants. A fair-trade, women's cooperative in Mexico creates bottles and pendants using dental tools. The tiny containers are unique works of art that mix glass and detailed ceramic work. The perfumes inside contain no alcohol or chemicals, and they have not been tested on animals. Michael O'Malley created a collection of 25 fragrances, but he is better known for his custom blends of individually tailored perfumes.

Your blending session begins with a conversation in O'Malley's comfortable office, full of plants and lined with shelves of essential oils. He will ask you what scents you like and what you've worn in the past. Then, with your permission, he smells you to determine your natural odor. He then offers scents for you to smell to narrow down your preferences. Using his inventory of 350 essential oils and fragrance compounds, he blends a perfume to harmonize with your natural chemistry. He may create three or four different blends using as few as two or three ingredients or as many as 25 for you to choose from.

O'Malley was once a math teacher. Then, he fell in love with the art of perfumery while travelling, and it turned out he had a knack for it. After studying for four years, he opened a small shop in Osborne Village in 1993. He moved to his current location in the Wolseley neighbourhood in 1999. Initially, 80 per cent of his customers were women, but over the years, more men have become interested. He says men now make up about 40 per cent of his customer base.

A gentle, pleasant aroma fills the space at La Parfumerie. It doesn't overpower. It simply encourages you to browse the fragrance selection and perhaps create your own signature scent.

Address 145 Evanson Street, Winnipeg, MB R3G 2A1, +1 (204) 475-4895, www.nothingperfume.com | **Getting there** Bus 11, 21, or 24 to Portage & Burnell (Stop 10552) or Portage & Arlington (Stop 10573) | **Hours** Thu–Sat noon–6pm or by appointment | **Tip** Visit Tall Grass Prairie Bread Company for breads made with their own heritage organic milled wheat flour, cinnamon buns, or other sweet treats (859 Westminster Avenue, www.tallgrassbakery.ca).

58 Leatherdale Centre
Polar bear conservation and rescue

Underwater tunnels, pool enclosures, rugged landscape, and shaded dens offer splendid polar bear viewing at Assiniboine Park Zoo's "Journey to Churchill" exhibit. Most of the bears here were rescued from the wild as orphaned cubs.

To learn more about polar bear conservation and the rescue of orphaned cubs, visit the interpretive centre at neighbouring Leatherdale International Polar Bear Conservation Centre (IPBCC), a hub for wildlife education, research, and conservation. Interactive displays provide information on the Arctic ecosystem, climate change, melting sea ice, and other challenges facing the polar bear population, as well as conservation efforts. Push the buttons to learn about subjects that interest you, and experts provide answers via pre-recorded videos. Play the games to find out ways you can reduce your impact on the environment.

Churchill, located along Hudson's Bay in northern Manitoba, is the polar bear capital of the world. The bears, recognized as an important part of the province's natural heritage and culture, are a protected species. They are brought into human care only under special circumstances. Displays at the Interpretive Centre explain what makes a cub a candidate for rescue and highlight the rescue and transition processes. Cubs undergo a 30-day quarantine period at IPBCC, and positive reinforcement training helps them transition to life under human care. The bears then become part of Assiniboine Park Zoo or are moved to other accredited facilities. Sadly, orphaned cubs raised in human care would not survive life back in the wild.

Back at the Journey to Churchill exhibit, you'll have an even greater appreciation and understanding of the bears who frolic, feed, and play in the expansive habitats, which include Sea Ice Passage, an underwater tunnel where visitors can marvel at the polar bears swimming overhead.

Address 2595 Roblin Boulevard, Winnipeg, MB R3P 2N7, +1 (204) 927-6000, www.assiniboinepark.ca, info@assiniboineapark.ca | Getting there Bus 79 to Roblin & Zoo (Stops 60476/60477) | Hours See website for seasonal hours | Tip Find uniquely decorated, concrete bears created for a 2005 Manitoba Cancercare fundraiser on the Manitoba Legislative Building's south grounds (450 Broadway Avenue, www.gov.mb.ca/legislature).

59 Living Prairie Museum
Tall grass prairie in the midst of the city

Only one per cent of the tall grass prairie that once covered more than one million square kilometres (over 386,000 square miles) of central North America remains. A small patch exists in the midst of a city residential area at the Living Prairie Museum, offering a glimpse into the landscape before European settlement.

The lawns of non-native grass in the surrounding neighbourhood, visible along the preserve's outskirts, look very different from what you see along the self-guided trail here. The preserve's rich diversity includes more than 150 grass and wildflower species. You'll see many silver-coloured plants, as silver reflects the sun's light and helps plants stay cool and retain moisture. What's blooming depends on when you visit. See wild rose and purple prairie clover blooming in June. Showy goldenrod and asters bloom in August. In summer, butterflies and dragonflies flit by. The path is a good spot for bird watching, too.

The Living Prairie Museum is one of three Winnipeg sites on Manitoba's Pine to Prairie International Birding Trail. Don't be surprised if a prairie dog crosses your path, and if you visit in July, you might also see sheep, which are brought in for two to three weeks to graze and help with vegetation management. Use the guide booklet, available via download or at the front entrance, to discover more secrets of the tallgrass prairie.

Displays in the Interpretive Centre, open in summer months and for special events at other times of the year, provide more information about the prairie ecosystem. The Microscope Station allows you to take a closer look at the shapes, textures, and colours of tallgrass prairie specimens. In the playground/park next to the museum, at the north end of Prairie View Drive, you'll find the Living Prairie Museum Medicine Garden, featuring sage and sweetgrass, two of the four Indigenous sacred medicines.

Address 2795 Ness Avenue, Winnipeg, MB R3J 3S4, +1 (204) 832-0167, www.winnipeg.ca | Getting there Bus 24 to Ness & Prairie View (Stops 20159/20175) | Hours Trail: Daily dawn–dusk; Interpretive Centre: daily 10am–5pm July & Aug, Sat 10am–5pm May, June & Sept | Tip Visit Prairie Originals, specialists in growing native plants for landscaping, to get native prairie plants to add to your own garden (27 Bunns Road, Selkirk, www.prairieoriginals.com).

60 Louis Riel Statue

Controversial statue of a controversial figure

An abstract bronze statue by Manitoba artist Marcien Lemay (1926–2005) at French-language Université de Saint-Boniface features a naked and distorted Louis Riel (1844–1885). Two semi-circular concrete walls, designed by eminent Manitoba architect Étienne Gaboury (1930–2022), surround the statue and display quotations from Riel's writings. This statue has been as controversial as its subject and his portrayal in history.

Federal and provincial governments formally recognized Riel's contribution to Canada in 1992, and the 2023 Manitoba Louis Riel Act gave him the honorary title of "First Premier of Manitoba." But for many years, Riel was considered a traitor. He was a Métis leader, who advocated for their land, language, and political rights. His leadership in the Red River Resistance of 1869–1870 led to Manitoba becoming Canada's fifth province. Elected three times to the House of Commons – and twice expelled for his role in the Resistance – he was forced into exile in 1875. In 1884, the Métis in what is now Saskatchewan invited him to help fight for their rights in the North-West Rebellion. In 1885, the Canadian government convicted him of high treason. He was hanged in Regina.

This sculpture was originally on the grounds of the Manitoba Legislative Building. When unveiled in December 1971, Lemay said he wanted to express "the mood and suffering of a man sacrificing himself for his beliefs," according to the Manitoba Historical Society. Some thought it a shameful and inappropriate way to commemorate such an important leader. Others said it represented Riel's tortured soul and his being stripped naked by the government of the day. Debate continued for decades until the statue was replaced in 1995 with a more statesman-like statue by Miguel Joyal, in which Riel wears a suit and tie. The original was moved to the Université de Saint-Boniface in 1995.

Address 200 De la Cathédrale Avenue, Winnipeg, MB R2H 0H7, +1 (204) 233-0210, www.ustboniface.ca, info@ustboniface.ca | Getting there Bus 10 to Aulneau & De La Cathedrale (Stops 50181/50182) | Hours Unrestricted | Tip The art gallery of the Franco-Manitobain Cultural Centre stages 4 to 6 exhibitions a year and is free to visit (340 Provencher Boulevard, www.ccfm.mb.ca/lagaleriedartduccfm).

61 MAKE Coffee + Stuff

Design, culture, coffee, and conversation

MAKE Coffee + Stuff features plain wooden tables, tall white walls, and a coffee/espresso counter at the back. This is a coffee shop, but it is also more than a coffee shop. It is an architecture and design exhibition space, a spot where you can read or study, and a place for discussion.

In 17th-century London, "Penny Universities" were coffee houses where people of all backgrounds (though mostly men) engaged in intellectual discussions for the price of admission and coffee, which was a penny at the time. Along that same vein, MAKE fosters free and open debate in a respectful space. Jae-Sung Chon, a full-time member of the University of Manitoba Faculty of Architecture, opened the shop in 2012 to showcase students' work, as there were few other such opportunities.

MAKE hosts exhibitions and design events. White walls provide display space, and ceiling racks allow for hanging exhibits. One exhibition featured winners of an international lamp shade contest. Notice a wooden map of the city at the front, created by a former student for Nuit Blanche, with rolled-up bits of paper dangling from pegs on the map, inviting you to trade favourite memories of specific city sites. A postcard gallery featuring photos of design projects got its start during the COVID-19 pandemic, when the faculty's annual Year End Exhibition of student work was suspended. Friends and family members could view students' creations as they waited in line, socially distanced, to pick up their coffee.

Chon calls MAKE "a for-profit enterprise run in a non-profit manner." You can buy architecture and design books, note paper, coloured drawing pencils, and coffee merchandise at the back of the shop. Proceeds go back into the shop to support exhibitions and student art. The coffee shop venue encourages interaction and conversation during events or any time you drop in. Background music is kept low.

Address 751 Corydon Avenue, Winnipeg, MB R3M 0W5, +1 (204) 414-0101, www.makecoffee.ca, info@makecoffee.ca | **Getting there** Bus 18 to Corydon & Cockburn (stops 10143/10144) | **Hours** Tue–Thu 9am–10pm, Fri–Mon 9am–7pm | **Tip** In Enderton Park, better known as "Peanut Park," stone markers in border flower beds identify the name of the community member maintaining that bit of garden (11 Ruskin Row, www.winnipeg.ca).

62 Manitoba Electrical Museum

A travelling kitchen promotes electricity

When even a short power outage disrupts our lives today, it's hard to imagine a time when people didn't want to use electricity. Manitoba Electrical Museum's 1940s Farm Kitchen speaks to such a time.

After World War II, plans to bring electricity to 50,000 farms by 1955 meant the installation of thousands of kilometres of transmission and distribution lines. This effort provided employment for men returning from the war, but it was a costly enterprise. To keep electricity prices low, at least 65 per cent of farms in an area needed to sign up. The power company undertook initiatives to encourage them to do so. They set up kitchens, such as the one on display, in host farms on Farm Field Days. A power company home economist showed farm wives how to use kitchen appliances like the ones you'll see here. Outside, company men demonstrated electric tools and farm equipment to the husbands.

Exhibit signage welcomes you to Elizabeth's kitchen. In 1948, Elizabeth Goulding worked as the power company home economist, promoting the use of electricity. A column she wrote for an electric bill pamphlet included recipes, homemaking hints, and tips on using electric appliances. The next two home economists were also named Elizabeth. Their role became known as "The Elizabeth."

Exhibits at the Manitoba Electrical Museum show the evolution of appliances and the use of electricity in the province. After seeing displays about the building of the hydroelectric generating stations that supply 95 per cent of Manitoba's power and the installation of power lines, you'll better understand the elaborate measures taken to sell people on the use of electricity. The company came close to meeting its targets. In 1955, 48,000 farms and 320 towns in southern Manitoba had electricity, and, as the museum display says, *the arrival of electricity changed life on the farm forever.*

Address 680 Harrow Street, Winnipeg, MB R3M 3A3, +1 (204) 360-7905, www.electricalmuseum.ca, info@electricalmuseum.ca | Getting there Bus 60 to Pembina & Stafford (Stops 10085/10086) | Hours Tue–Sat 1–4pm | Tip Stock your modern kitchen with fun and functional cookware, bakeware, knives, dishes, and gadgets from d.a. Niels Gourmet Kitchenware (485 Berry Street, www.danielsgourmetkitchenware.ca).

63 Manitoba Hydro Place

Energy-efficient office tower of the future

The signature architecture of Manitoba Hydro Place, which opened in downtown Winnipeg in 2009, features a splayed twin glass office tower 22 storeys high, but its most unique aspects are not blatantly visible. The LEED Platinum-certified building housing the headquarters of Manitoba's electricity and natural gas utility is one of North America's most energy-efficient and green office towers, using 70% less energy than a comparable office building of conventional design.

The building was designed to be an energy-efficient, sustainable, and healthy workplace. It was also designed for Winnipeg's climate. A geothermal system taps energy stored in the ground for heating and cooling. South-facing winter gardens optimized solar exposure, and a solar chimney takes advantage of the environment and natural processes to reduce energy usage. Atria located throughout the building act as solar collectors and air exchangers. They also provide staff with comfortable rest spaces and meeting areas. Atria water features regulate humidity. Other building characteristics include a raised-floor displacement ventilation system, exposed radiant concrete ceilings that maintain building temperatures, low-iron glass that maximizes the amount of natural daylight, energy-efficient lighting and pumps, and a living green roof.

An impressive main floor gallery is accessible to the public. The three-storey-high area houses the building's main entrance, serves as a sheltered pedestrian route between Portage and Graham Avenues, and provides space for community events. Bison sculptures stand at both entrances. Tall plants line the walls. Two wall waterfalls cascading over a granite surface replicate the spillway of a hydroelectric generating station and help regulate humidity. A landscaped public courtyard and park along Graham Avenue is home to a weekly farmers' market in summer.

Address 360 Portage Avenue, Winnipeg, MB R3C 0G8, +1 (204) 480-5900, www.hydro.mb.ca | Getting there Bus 10, 11, 14, 15, 19, 21, 24, 38, 43, or 55 to Portage & Edmonton (Stops 10543/10581) or Portage & Carlton (Stop 10527) | Hours Daily 6am–6pm | Tip Hargrave St. Market is an upscale food hall featuring food and drink from some of Winnipeg's best chefs and restaurant groups (242 Hargrave Street, www.hargravestmarket.com).

64　Manitoba Museum
The first Black labour union in North America

The Manitoba Museum holds the human and natural history of the province, from ancient to contemporary times. In 1970, the museum, then called Museum of Man and Nature, opened in its current location and has added galleries over time.

Opened in 2019, the Winnipeg Gallery holds local history and artifacts, such as a stained-glass Winnipeg sign that was at the old City Hall and displays exploring various themes in Winnipeg's history. The Personalities Wall here tells the stories of 30 citizens who've contributed to the city since the 1870s to the present day, including John Arthur Robinson.

Born in the West Indies, Robinson came to Winnipeg around 1909. He worked as a sleeping car porter, one of the few jobs available to Black men at the time. Porters attended to every need of sleeping-car travellers. Without their own sleeping quarters, they grabbed naps when they could, even during trips that could last three days, according to a story by the CBC. They earned less than their white colleagues. They paid for their own uniforms, shoeshine kits, and meals. They could be fired at any time without reason. Railway unions of the day did not allow Black members.

In 1917, Robinson and three other porters formed their own union. The Order of Sleeping Car Porters was the first Black labour union in North America. They negotiated contracts with the Canadian National Railway in 1919. Canadian Pacific Railway was more resistant and, in the 1920s, dismissed porters involved in unions. It took until 1945 to gain a collective bargaining agreement. Robinson retired in 1947 and returned to St. Kitts, where he died in 1950.

The museum's other galleries are also well worth visiting for the first time or an overdue re-visit. Galleries have been updated as part of a major renewal project, with special attention to the stories of Indigenous Peoples and new Canadians.

Address 190 Rupert Avenue, Winnipeg, MB R3B 0N2, +1 (204) 956-2830, www.manitobamuseum.ca, info@manitobamuseum.ca | Getting there Bus 11, 15, 16, 18, 20, 21, 24, 44, 45, or 47 to Main & James (Stops 10629/10634) | Hours Tue – Sun 10am – 4pm | Tip Visit the Nonsuch Brewing Co. taproom, a four-minute walk away, to try award-winning Belgian and European ales. Be sure to order the fermented potato chips (125 Pacific Avenue, www.nonsuch.beer).

65 Manitoba Sports Hall of Fame

Honouring Manitoba's athletes through history

The Manitoba Sports Hall of Fame, located in the Sport Manitoba building, preserves the province's rich history of athleticism and sports. Take plenty of time to look through all the cases containing memorabilia, photographs, and textual information group sport stories by decade. You'll find clothing from special sporting events, equipment, medals, banners, and touching congratulatory telegrams among the many items here. Exhibits cover a wide variety of sports and leagues, including baseball, basketball, bowling, cricket, curling, cycling, golf, skiing, tennis, and, of course, hockey.

Hockey certainly takes pride of place here. Look for the well-worn skates that belonged to Charlie Johnstone of the Winnipeg Victorias, the men's hockey team that won the Stanley Cup in 1896, 1901, and 1902, and the banquet program celebrating the Falcon Hockey Club's 1920 Olympics gold-medal win. The Winnipeg Falcons team was formed in 1910 with players of Icelandic descent, who were not allowed to play on other teams due to racial prejudice. They represented Canada in the 1920 Olympics in Antwerp, Belgium, where hockey was first declared an Olympic sport.

The Avco World Trophy is the actual presentation cup of the World Hockey Association, the professional ice hockey major league that operated in North America from 1972 to 1979. The Winnipeg Jets won that trophy three times, more wins than any other league team.

Other displays throughout the museum space, including the lobby, feature temporary exhibits that change regularly, as the Sports Hall of Fame has 10,000 items in its archive. Before you leave, take the elevator to the second floor, where you'll find a mural of the Winnipeg Falcons 1920 Hockey Club painted by local artist Luther Pokrant in 2002.

Address 145 Pacific Avenue, Winnipeg, MB R3B 2Z6, +1 (204) 925-5936, www.sportmanitoba.ca/hall-of-fame, halloffame@sportmanitoba.ca | Getting there Bus 11, 15, 16, 18, 20, 44, 45, or 47 to Main & James (Stops 10629/10634) or bus 21 or 24 to Pacific & Martha (Stop 10800) | Hours Tue–Fri 11am–3pm | Tip A plaque at the First Lutheran Church, established by the Icelandic community in 1878, commemorates the Falcons, many of whom were members (580 Victor Street).

66 Manitoboggan
Stylish and accessible toboggan slide

Amidst the trees in St. Vital Park, you'll find a stylish, Douglas fir-sided structure that looks like something from a design magazine. It's a toboggan slide that allows people of all abilities to embrace winter.

Designed for the city of Winnipeg by Public City Architecture, Manitoboggan offers two slides, one of which is fully accessible. It also features a treetop lookout and a shelter. A steel feature wall has V-shaped cutouts in a design inspired by an iconic sweater pattern by Mary Maxim, the family-owned needlework company that first began in Sifton, Manitoba in 1937 as a woolen mill. Manitoboggan has received two Olympic Committee awards and an Award of Excellence from the Canadian Society of Landscape Architects.

Manitoboggan opened in 2017 to replace previous slides and a warming shelter destroyed by fire in 2013. Its two slide chutes sit at different levels. The lower slide has a gradual slope on the way down, while the upper slide is steeper. An accessible ramp meanders through the trees to a viewing platform and the slides. The ramp was developed with the existing forest in mind – no trees were removed during construction. There is space at the launch to transfer from a wheelchair to a sled. In a December 2017 *Winnipeg Free Press* article, Paralympian Billy Bridges, who made the inaugural slide, said the ramp was easy to use, and the slide was a lot of fun. Both slides end with a gradual wind-down and slip into a stand of trees. A cozy warming shelter with benches and heaters sits under the deck of the lower slide.

In a city known for its flat terrain, toboggan slides create hills for sledding fun. The stylish Manitoboggan makes that hill accessible to all. Its unique design is impressive to see even when there isn't snow on the ground. You can visit the treetop lookout year-round, and the warming shelter becomes a picnic shelter in summer months.

Address 190 River Road, Winnipeg, MB, parkmaps.winnipeg.ca | **Getting there** Bus 676 to River & Kilmarnock South (Stops 50396/50397) | **Hours** Daily 7:30am–10pm | **Tip** Jumpstart Playground is fully accessible with barrier-free entry, double-wide ramps, and static-free roller slides that won't compromise hearing devices (25 Poseidon Bay).

67 — Marshall McLuhan Home
The medium is the message

In the 1960s, decades before the era of social media, Marshall McLuhan, who was a pioneer in media analysis and famous for his provocative theories, coined the phrase, "The medium is the message." He spoke of the "global village" and saw it as a loss of individuality and privacy. His 1962 non-fiction book *The Gutenberg Galaxy* won a Governor General's Award, and he became a Companion of the Order of Canada in 1970. He appeared briefly in Woody Allen's 1977 movie *Annie Hall*. His face was on a 2000 Canadian postage stamp. In 2008, he received a National Historic Persons designation because of the insights and tools he provided to make sense of the electronic age.

Born in Edmonton in 1911, McLuhan moved to Winnipeg with his family in 1915. He grew up in the city and studied at the University of Manitoba, where he received a BA in English and Philosophy and a master's degree. He received a PhD from Cambridge University in 1942 and was a professor of English Literature at the University of Toronto from 1942 until 1979. McLuhan died in 1980.

The family home in which McLuhan grew up still stands. The modest, two-and-a-half-storey house with a covered front veranda is more remarkable for its former resident than any particular detail or structural feature. McLuhan lived here for 19 years – formative years that would have shaped his thinking. McLuhan never forgot his Winnipeg roots. In a 1974 conversation with Danny Finkleman of the Canadian Broadcasting Corporation, he spoke of the beauty of the Western (prairie) skies, stating, "The Westerner doesn't have a point of view. He has a vast panorama." McLuhan called Winnipeggers "Winnipigeons."

In 1967, McLuhan was awarded an Honorary Doctor of Letters from the University of Manitoba, where a banquet room bears his name. He was inducted into the Winnipeg Regional Real Estate Board's Citizens Hall of Fame in 2019.

Address 507 Gertrude Avenue, Winnipeg, MB R3L 0M7 | **Getting there** Bus 16, 18, or 60 to Osborne & Osborne Junction (Stops 10066/10067/10068) | **Hours** Viewable from the outside only | **Tip** Bronze busts on pedestals in Citizens Hall of Fame at Assiniboine Park honour those who've contributed to Winnipeg's quality of life with outstanding achievements (2355 Corydon Avenue, www.assiniboinepark.ca).

68 MICEC

Indigenous art, culture, and history on display

The Manitoba Indigenous Cultural Education Centre Inc. (MICEC) was formed in 1975 to reclaim Indigenous cultures, languages, and education. They offer language classes, presentations, and art and craft workshops. Over the years, the centre has also amassed over 1,000 pieces of artwork and other artifacts of historical and cultural importance in the Heritage Collection, much of which is displayed throughout the centre.

Outside MICEC is an eye-catching sculpture, a circle of seven huge, wooden poles representing Manitoba Indigenous languages. Animals on the poles symbolize different aspects of Indigenous culture. Step inside and look down to see the star blanket pattern inlaid in the wooden floors. Light streams through two levels of windows into the two-storey gathering space. Almond-coloured walls, display cases, and ledges showcase the collection. Items on display change regularly, but you're likely to see beaded costumes, carvings, drums, snowshoes, sacred medicines, dream catchers, ceremony regalia, stone tools, pottery, and paintings.

MICEC's collection started with a blank wall. The story is that a visiting artist convinced the staff to buy a set of six moon line drawings to add decoration, and things took off from there. On the half-walled mezzanine level, you'll find a lending library with over 14,000 volumes, photos, and audio recordings covering all aspects of Indigenous culture. Don't miss the children's area alcove with many books for young readers and a starry night painting in the domed ceiling by Shawna Boulette Grapentine.

The 2010 renovation of MICEC's building, originally constructed in 1902 for All People's Mission, earned a Heritage Winnipeg Preservation Award and created a warm and welcoming space for MICEC programs and its one-of-a-kind collection. First-time visitors are awe-struck by its beauty and the collection of art.

Address 119 Sutherland Avenue, Winnipeg, MB R2W 3C9, +1 (204) 942-0228, www.micec.com, info@micec.com | Getting there Bus 45 to Euclid & Argyle (Stops 30434/30545) | Hours Mon–Fri 8:30am–4:30pm, see MICEC's Facebook page for events | Tip The artist-run Urban Shaman gallery of contemporary aboriginal art presents contemporary Indigenous art while remaining rooted in traditional cultures (203-290 McDermot Avenue, www.urbanshaman.org).

69   Mulvey Market
Winnipeg's largest year-round indoor flea market

Mulvey Market's 40+ vendors sell a vast variety of new and gently used products, vintage items, and antiques. You'll find basketball and hockey star cards, toys, action figures, board games, china, tools, jewelry, incense, cowboy hats, belts, jackets, and pickles. There are collectibles like porcelain figurines and soda pop bottles. Look for one-of-a-kind miniatures and unusual lamps made from industrial parts. Add to your music collection from a selection of vinyl, CDs, and cassette tapes. Collect *Star Wars* and Coca-Cola memorabilia. Choose an old tin sign or order a personalized one. Antiques may include radio cabinets, shelves, clocks, or even a gramophone.

Take your time browsing the eclectic mix of items. The treasure that speaks to you may be hidden among jam-packed shelves. You might find old rotary dial phones wired for current use or a skull-shaped lava lamp. A 1960s-era table-top hockey game may evoke nostalgia in older visitors. Vendors gladly explain the purpose and use of vintage items to younger folk who have not seen them before.

You'll also find a selection of collectible trading card games and supplies. Mulvey Market hosts Pokémon trading nights several times a year, usually shortly after new releases. Kids of all ages, gather to trade cards or buy new ones. Staff members supervise the events, ensuring fair trading and an enjoyable experience for everyone.

You need to go around the market more than once to take in everything. Should you need sustenance while shopping, stop at the canteen. Food items include burgers, hot dogs, nachos, poutine, and bagels. It is a delight to browse through Mulvey Market, whether you buy or not. However, chances are you will not leave empty-handed. There is something for everyone at Winnipeg's largest year-round indoor flea market and different treasures to find each time you visit.

Address 421 Mulvey Avenue East, Winnipeg, MB R3L 0R6, +1 (204) 990-4049, www.mulveymarket.com | Getting there Bus 16 to Osborne & Mulvey (Stops 10001/ 10065) | Hours Sat & Sun & long weekends/holidays 10am – 5pm | Tip Enjoy food, drink, live music, a welcoming neighbourhood bar vibe, and perhaps even a game of bowling while the music plays at Park Alleys (730 Osborne Street, www.parkalleys.com).

70_ Naval Museum of Manitoba

Honouring the prairie sailors

You might not expect to find a naval unit in a prairie city thousands of kilometres away from any of the three oceans bordering Canada, but, for some unexplained reason, the Canadian Navy has deep roots in Manitoba. HMCS Chippewa in Winnipeg houses a Royal Canadian Navy reserve division and a local recruitment centre. Inside its building, the Naval Museum of Manitoba showcases the province's naval heritage as well as the history of the Canadian Navy.

Displays include models of ships, medals, life rafts, artillery, and communications equipment. An exhibit of uniforms and insignia explain Navy ranks. There are shiny ship's bells, used to indicate the hour aboard a ship and regulate sailors' duty watches, and exhibits about women in the Navy. The "Three Princes" display highlights a unique part of Canada's World War II effort in which three mercantile ships were reconfigured to infantry landing ships and an anti-aircraft escort. More personal items, such as steins, furlough cards, and old cigarette packages, speak to sailors' lives beyond their duties. Other exhibits, panels, and newspaper clippings provide information about the Canadian Navy and Manitoba's role in it.

The Canadian Navy was formed in 1910, and a reserve division was established in Winnipeg in 1923. From 1939 to 1945, the World War II years, Manitoba residents who joined the Navy completed their basic training at HMCS Chippewa, which turned out a total of 7,736 men and women during that period. It was the third-largest Navy recruiting centre in Canada.

A bronze statue in front of HMCS Chippewa pays homage to the prairie sailors who served in the Battle of the Atlantic. *The Prairie Sailor*, created by Winnipeg artist Helen Granger Young, features a young seated sailor looking into the distance with his seabag at his side.

Address 1 Navy Way, Winnipeg, MB R3C 4J7, www.naval-museum.mb.ca, friends@naval-museum.mb.ca | Getting there Bus Blue, 14, 19, 47, or 55 to Main & Assiniboine (Stops 10624/10642) or 23 or 66 to Broadway & Garry (Stop 10590) or Broadway & Smith (Stop 10589) | Hours Wed 9am–3pm | Tip The always-open outdoor Air Force Air Park features a collection of military aircraft (186 Air Force Way).

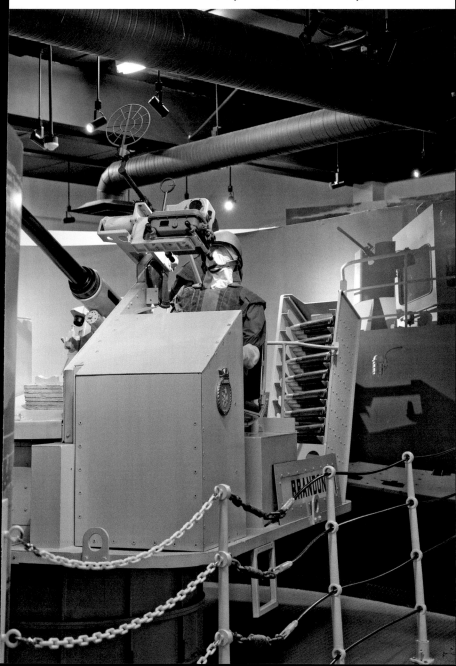

71 North Forge FabLab

Where ideas are transformed into something tangible

You need to see the advanced equipment at North Forge Technology Exchange's Fabrication Lab to appreciate it fully. Weekly tours of North America's largest, publicly accessible, non-profit fabrication lab offer that very opportunity. As you walk through this Safe Work-certified facility, you'll see carpentry and woodworking machines, laser cutters, an electronics laboratory, metalworking equipment, a water jet cutting table, 3D printers, specialty printers, computer-aided design resources, and more. When you tour the facility, you're likely to be as impressed as King Charles was on his 2014 visit.

After your tour, you might be considering joining the community through one of the many different options, starting with the free Pathfinder option to get you started. Among the diverse group of women and men working and learning here, you'll find Red Seal carpenters, students, startups, artists, engineers developing prototypes, retirees taking up artistic endeavours, and tinkerers. The range of equipment allows makers to put together all parts of their creations. For example, a custom knife maker forms the blades, makes wooden handles, laser cuts names into the handles, and creates colour graphic packaging. Many members volunteer their expertise to help other community members.

A chance meeting between two technology professionals at a TedX talk led to the lab's creation. With sponsorship from friendly companies and the help of enthusiastic volunteers, the lab opened in 2011. It has grown in space and capability over the years. North Forge is also a non-profit incubator accelerator helping startups in technology, STEM, and advanced manufacturing. That program offers entrepreneurs assistance to go from prototyping to commercialization.

If you find you're not a maker yourself, you'll enjoy shopping for handmade wares in the North Forge Lab's Makers Market shop.

Address 125 Adelaide Street, Winnipeg, MB R3A 0W4, +1 (204) 262 6400, www.northforge.ca, info@northforge.ca | **Getting there** Bus 12 or 23 to William & Princess (Stops 10721/10722) | **Hours** Tours: Tue 6pm; Makers Market: Tue – Fri 9am – 4pm; see website for events and trainings | **Tip** In the same building, the artist community Cre8ery Gallery & Studio exhibits and sells members' works and rents studio spaces, many of which are open to the public (125 Adelaide Street, www.cre8ery.com).

72__ The Old House Revival Co. & Antique Mall

Old objects, new treasures

Whether you're searching for a unique find for your home restoration project, shopping for vintage decor, looking for a trip down memory lane, or simply browsing through an eclectic collection, The Old House Revival Co. & Antique Mall is the place to go.

Housed in a historic, early-twentieth-century warehouse, the mall carries architectural salvaged items, antique furniture, and much more. Everything is so artfully arranged on the large main floor – you won't know where to look first. Vintage appliances, antiques, and curios form attractive vignettes. Bins contain decorative door handles and hinges. The store is known for its extensive lighting collection, and chandeliers and other fixtures hang from ladders attached horizontally to the high ceiling. There are stained-glass windows and panels. Large items, such as tables and cabinets dating from the 1930s and earlier, stand throughout the space. You'll find china, ornaments, cookware, collectibles, tools, toys, and curiosities sitting on tables and shelves.

The extensively renovated building oozes charm. Tin tiles dot the ceiling. The beautiful wood on the wall behind the cash desk comes from a collection of old doors. Mixed in with the many items for sale are a few one-of-a-kind ones that are not for sale items but displayed solely for interest. Those include an old Winnipeg Police call box, the front half of an old car chassis tucked into a ledge near the ceiling, and a large bird cage in one corner containing a life-sized skeleton.

On the other floors, 40 vendors display a wide variety of antiques and vintage wares. The store is a delight to stroll through. If you didn't start out specifically shopping for something, there is a good chance you'll be taking something home with you.

Address 324 Young Street, Winnipeg, MB R3B 2S4, +1 (204) 477-4286, www.theoldhouserevival.com, theoldhousestaff@gmail.com | **Getting there** Bus 11 or 55 to Portage & Langside (Stops 10547/10578) | **Hours** Tue–Sun 10am–4pm | **Tip** Stop at the nearby Junior's Restaurant for a Fat Burger, an iconic Winnipeg beef burger containing condiments, cheddar cheese, and chili meat (558 Portage Avenue, www.juniorswinnipeg.com).

73__Pete's Center Canada Heritage Museum

Open-air museum of antique farm equipment

As you drive the Trans-Canada Highway past the longitudinal centre of Canada, a little east of Winnipeg, you'll see a farmyard of antique farm equipment and vehicles. The field at Pete's Centre of Canada Heritage Museum has been landscaped to show off the pieces and provide photo opportunities. Berms become display cases, and plantings of trees create backdrops. You'll find a central pond, picnic tables, farm machines, and agricultural implements of varying ages.

Pierre Pelland maintains the attraction at his own expense as a way to celebrate the centre of Canada. Since starting work on the museum around 2011 and buying the first plough, his collection has grown to over 150 pieces including dozens of vehicles. Pelland acquires pieces through auctions and classified ads, mostly from within an 80-kilometre (50-mile) radius. Grandchildren can visit and see pieces that once belonged to their grandparents. The equipment sits on display and weathers the elements. When asked what his favourites were, Pelland said, "The rustier the better."

A walk through the field can be a treasure hunt to look for the oldest pieces. A 1918 Ford tractor and an 1878 potato digger are among the oldest, but no signage identifies vintage or history. Those familiar with farm machinery can use serial numbers and manufacturer markings to date pieces, but you needn't be farm-machine-savvy to appreciate the museum. You'll see the evolution of farming techniques in the differences from horse-drawn to tractor-pulled equipment, and from steel wheels to rubber tires. And in the variety of engines, you'll notice increasing complexity of operation and the improvements in seating comfort. There are even some items for sale should you be interested in adding rustic yard art to your home.

Address 52063 Municipal Road 28 E, Rosewood, MB R5K 0H3, +1 (204) 878-9002 | Getting there By car, drive east on Highway 1 to where Provincial Road 206 South joins the highway, turn north and then west on Stuart Road to the junction of Stuart Road and Road 28 East | Hours Daily dawn–dusk | Tip Take a selfie at the "Centre of Canada" billboard in neighbouring Centre of Canada Park, which also offers a picnic area, playground, and interpretive plaques (R.M. of Taché, www.centreofcanada.ca).

74 Pilehenge
Cement cemetery

In a field on the northern outskirts of Winnipeg, but still within the Perimeter Highway, grey concrete pillars of varying heights and laid out in a grid rise from the tops of four circular mounds grouped in pairs. The concrete piles are between 15 to 18 metres (50 to 60 feet) in length. What are these odd-looking structures? Are they something created by or for extraterrestrials? Is this a site of occult worship? Both theories have been part of the speculation about the site's origin. Because the formation may bring Stonehenge to mind, people have dubbed it Pilehenge. Does it, like Stonehenge, track the movement of the sun, the moon, and the stars?

The answer may be less mysterious. According to the Manitoba Historical Society, this is an abandoned industrial site. The British-American Cement Company planned to build a cement factory here. They began driving concrete piles into the ground in November 1963. Numbers written into the concrete when wet represent the date the pile was created and its length. Another company, Inland Cement, also had plans to build a new cement factory in Winnipeg. Two new cement plants, in addition to the existing Canada Cement plant, were more than Manitoba needed. In April 1964, the City of Winnipeg decided to give all of their cement business to Inland. Shortly thereafter, Inland purchased the British-American Cement Company site, which was abandoned when Inland built their new plant in a different location.

The two mounds nearest Sturgeon Road are the largest. From the road, you may notice bits of graffiti on some of the pillars. A closer look requires walking through a ditch and tall grass in the summer or trudging through snow in winter. The cement cemetery from any viewpoint exudes eeriness. Even with knowing its earthly industrial history, you can easily let your imagination run a little wild and conjure up otherworldly forces that could be at play here.

Address Sturgeon Road, Rosser, MB R0H 1E0 | Getting there By car, drive on Inkster Boulevard to Wheatfield Road, turn north and then immediately west onto Park Royale Way, turn north onto Sturgeon Road at the end of Royale Way. Pilehenge is on the west side of the road. | Hours Unrestricted | Tip Enjoy a summer weekend themed excursion on the Prairie Dog Central, a 1900-era vintage train (64099 Prairie Dog Trail, Rosser, www.pdcrailway.com).

75 Pollock Island

The island park that isn't always an island

Pollock Island, one of Winnipeg's lesser-known parks, isn't usually an island. Nestled in a 6.5-hectare (16 acre) plot of land in St. Norbert. where the La Salle and Red Rivers meet, the park becomes an island only when flood waters are high.

A gravel, 1.3-kilometre (0.8-mile), circular trail runs through the park. On the tree and fern-lined path into the park, you see the river on both sides of you, visible only in glimpses through the leaves in summer. In a few minutes, you become surrounded by dense riverbottom forest. Here you'll find giant cottonwood trees, old basswoods, wild vines, and berry bushes. Riverbottom forests, one of the most diverse wildlife habitats on the prairies, are increasingly rare. The Pollock Island Conservation Group and the City of Winnipeg Naturalist Services work together to protect the area's biodiversity.

Interpretive panels provide information on the flora and fauna as well as the park's history. The park, which feels natural and untouched, has had a busy history. Woodland hunters stalked deer thousands of years ago. Traders came from far away to broker deals. Bison hunters met here before a hunt. Fur traders camped. Winnipeggers picnicked here in the 1800s. Around 1945, Tina Pollock bought the land from the Roman Catholic Parish of St. Norbert. Initially, she came to Pollock Island only on weekends to garden. In 1957, her son Edward and his wife Iris moved into a house that had been built on the property the previous year. Pollock visited often and stayed in a small cottage beside the house. In 2006, she donated the property to the people of Winnipeg as an eco-gift, the first ever in the city.

The trail, considered to be relatively easy, is open year-round for hiking, walking, and snowshoeing. Keep your eyes open for birds and deer. At one point, you'll have a view in the distance of the Red River Floodway gates.

Address 200 St. Pierre Street, Winnipeg, MB, www.mhs.mb.ca/docs/sites/pollockisland.shtml | Getting there Bus 91 to De L'Église & St. Pierre (Stop 60753), walk to the southern end of St. Pierre Street | Hours Unrestricted | Tip Sentier Cloutier Trail, part of Trans Canada Trail, also goes past riverbottom forest as well as a mature tree nursery (Cloutier Drive, www.winnipegtrails.ca).

76 Pollock's Hardware
The little hardware store that could

You may feel as if you've stepped back in time when you visit Pollock's Hardware Co-op Ltd. The display window beside the front door contains a jumbled collection of old bottles, vintage tools, and crates. You'll even find a granite curling stone and a World War I helmet in the mix. Inside, the well-worn, wooden floor creaks under your steps, and pressed tin tiles adorn the ceiling. Bins contain loose nails and bolts sold by weight. Other traditional hardware items, along with a mix of housewares, toys, cleaning products, garden supplies, and specialty items, create the feel of an old-time general store.

Pollock's has a long history. It opened as a general hardware store in 1922 and quickly became a neighbourhood institution. People gathered here. In the early days, they listened to hockey games on the radio. Then-owners Wayne and Lois Cash closed the store in 2007 when they wanted to retire and had been unable to find a buyer for the business. Dismayed community members hated to see the north-end icon shut down. They held meetings and reopened the store in 2008 as a cooperative.

The store nearly closed again in 2019 due to financial difficulties, but members overwhelmingly voted to keep the store open.

Pollock's still carries an eclectic mix of products, including a number of locally made and rare items used to fix old houses. A crokinole board hangs on the wall. Look for the extensive collection of vintage Pyrex. The house plants decorating the shelves are for sale. If you remember potted plants at your grandmother's or great-aunt's house resting on saucers, check out the stack of old saucers sold individually as drip trays.

Take your time to browse. You'll find unexpected treasures, from vintage toys, to local souvenirs, to Beeproject North End Neighbourhood Honey, to perogi makers. Pollock's Hardware remains a community institution.

Address 1407 Main Street, Winnipeg, MB R2W 3V2, +1 (204) 582-5007, www.pollockshardwarecoop.com, manager@phco-op.ca | Getting there Bus 18 to Main & Cathedral (Stops 30062/30071) | Hours Mon–Fri 10am–6pm, Sat 9am–6pm, Sun noon–5pm | Tip If you want perogies but prefer not to make your own, head to Luda's Deli for North End style perogies (410 Aberdeen Avenue).

77 Pooh Gallery
Winnie-the-Pooh's Winnipeg story

Assiniboine Park's distinctive Pavilion houses several free art spaces, including the cozy Pooh Gallery about the popular stuffed bear of children's fiction and his Winnipeg connection.

Author A. A. Milne's son Christopher Robin named his teddy bear Winnie after a black bear in the London Zoo. That teddy bear inspired Milne to create Winnie-the-Pooh, who lived in the Hundred Acre Wood with a cast of characters based on his son's other beloved toys, along with a fictionalized version of his son in his stories. *When We Were Young*, the first of Milne's books about the bear's adventures, was published in 1924. The character of Winnie-the-Pooh is male, but the real-life Winnie was female.

Harry Colebourn (1887–1947) was a veterinarian who had immigrated to Canada from England. In 1914, while en route to join Europe's World War I efforts, he bought an orphaned bear cub from a hunter in White River, Ontario and named her after his adopted hometown of Winnipeg. He took the cub to England, where he donated her to the London Zoo before he left for the front. While doing graduate studies in London post-war, he often visited Winnie at the zoo. In 1920, Colebourn returned to Winnipeg for the rest of his life. Winnie stayed in London.

The Pooh Gallery tells Winnie's story through photos of her and Colebourn, *Winnie-the-Pooh* books, and memorabilia such as handmade toys, collectibles, and postcards of the original stuffed animals that inspired Milne. Books on a children's table are there to be opened.

At the back of the gallery, you'll find a 1930s painting by Ernest Howard Shepard, who illustrated Milne's books. This painting features Winnie-the-Pooh gazing lovingly at a honey pot. According to a CBC news article, this is Shepard's only known oil painting of his bear character. It was acquired at a Sotheby's auction in 2000, when intense bidding pushed the price to $243,000.

Address 55 Pavilion Crescent, Winnipeg, MB R3P 2N6, +1 (204) 927-6000, www.assiniboinepark.ca, info@assiniboinepark.ca | Getting there Bus 18 or 79 to Corydon & Shaftesbury (Stops 60471/60472) or bus 11 or 21 to Portage & Overdale (Stops 20212/20418) | Hours Summer: daily 9am–5pm; winter: daily 9am–4pm | Tip Nature Playground beside the Pavilion contains unique play areas, a whimsical garden, and a statue of Colebourn and Winnie-the-Pooh cub crafted by artist William Epp.

78 Pool of the Black Star
Manitoba Legislative Building's secret symbols

The Manitoba Legislative Building, which officially opened in 1920, incorporates Greek, Roman, and Egyptian architectural elements inside and out. You'll find something of interest everywhere you look. Particularly impressive are the Rotunda at the top of the Grand Staircase and the Pool of the Black Star below it.

The Rotunda provides a formal approach to the Legislative Assembly, with Corinthian columns rising to the base of a decorated dome. The geometric design in the marble floor is known as the Greek key and signifies the eternal quest for knowledge. A circular opening in the floor provides a view of the Pool of the Black Star on the floor of the level below. As you walk around the opening's limestone balustrade and look over the railing, the Pool of the Black Star always appears closer to you than to the other side, even though it's perfectly centred beneath the opening. It features an eight-pointed star in alternating solid black and marbled black that represent the altars of ancient Greeks. Sounds from all over the building converge at its centre – when you stand there and whisper, your voice seems to boom.

The balustrade measures 13 feet across, and there are 13 bulbs in the Rotunda lamps – the number 13 repeats throughout the building, perhaps because ancient Egyptians equated 13 with good luck or because ancient Romans and Greeks considered 13 bad luck, and the number would welcome good luck or dispel back luck here. Some attribute it to Freemasonry symbolism. The numbers 5 and 8 also repeat. Architectural historian Dr. Frank Albo studied the building for 10 years starting in 2001 and found coded messages and secret teachings. He describes the building as a modern reconstruction of King Solomon's Temple.

Look for the secret Freemasonry traditions hidden in plain sight here, or simply marvel at the elaborate designs within this remarkable building.

Address 450 Broadway Avenue, Winnipeg, MB R3C 0V8, +1 (204) 945-5813, www.gov.mb.ca/legislature, tour_reservation@leg.gov.mb.ca | Getting there Bus 16, 18, or 60 to Osborne & Broadway (Stops 10596/10599) or 10, 17, 20, or 23 to Broadway & Osborne East (Stops 10585/10870) | Hours July & Aug hourly tours daily 9am–4pm, Sept–June Fri 2pm | Tip The Winnipeg Law Courts National Historic Site of Canada was built between 1912 and 1916 in the Beaux Arts style to complement the Legislative Building (391 Broadway Avenue).

79 Porter-Milady Ghost Sign
Shining light on fading ghost signs

After sunset, light projections recreate ghost signs on a six-storey building in the Exchange District. The term "ghost sign" refers to the advertisements painted on brick buildings that were prevalent from the 1890s to the 1960s. Sometimes, a new sign was painted on top of an original one. As the newer sign faded over time, bits of the previous sign became visible. Signs showing multiple worn ads are known as palimpsests, and they provide glimpses into the past.

Light projections cycle through the Porter-Milady palimpsest. One sign here lists the products sold by Porter & Co., a wholesale crockery and china firm. It was painted in 1906 when the business moved into the building, where it remained until it ceased operations in 1943. A second sign advertises Milady Chocolates. The L. Galpern Candy Company, manufacturer's agents for Milady Chocolates, was founded in 1907 by Louis Galpern and moved into the building in 1943. The company closed in 1973.

Matt Cohen and Craig Winslow, from Winnipeg and Portland, Oregon, respectively, collaborated on this light installation. Cohen documents Winnipeg's rich collection of fading ads on his website and conducts ghost sign tours. His research includes studying old photographs, catalogues, and actual products to determine the colours on the original ads. Through Light Capsules, his historical restoration effort, artist and designer Winslow uses non-destructive light projection to revive hand-painted advertisements via a process known as "augmented restoration."

In 2017, Cohen and Winslow staged a one-night event in which they brought five ghost signs back to life. In 2022, they created the permanent Stobart Installation on the west side of 281 McDermot Avenue. It cycles through three ads and was the world's first permanent Light Capsules ghost sign installation. The Milady-Porter installation was launched in 2023.

Address 165 McDermot Avenue, Winnipeg, MB R3B 0S1, www.lightcapsules.app/no/27 | Getting there Bus 11, 15, 16, 18, 20, 21, 24, 44, 45, or 47 to Main & McDermot (Stops 10628/10636) or Main & Lombard (Stop 10637) | Hours Daily dusk–midnight | Tip During the day, visit Sam's Place, a coffee shop and social enterprise helping youth facing employment challenges get training and experience (140 Bannatyne Avenue, www.samsplacecoffee.com).

80 Qaumajuq

World's largest contemporary Inuit art collection

The undulating white granite façade of Qaumajuq, home to the largest public collection of contemporary Inuit art in the world, reflects the scale and curved forms of the Canadian Arctic. A wall of glass panes at ground level gives passersby a glimpse inside where the Visible Vault captures one's attention.

The Visible Vault is a unique feature of the museum. Encased in glass walls, the three-storey vault contains nearly 500 glass shelves holding close to 5,000 stone carvings representing all of the communities where there is Inuit art production. Curved walls in a circular shape allow you to walk around the entire vault. It is the second storey of the vault you see at museum ground level. Glass floors at one end of the vault allow you peer into the lower lever. That level is below ground and connects to the full Qaumajuq vault. A stairway leading up to Qaumajuq gallery spaces offers closer views of carvings in the Vault's top storey. The Visible Vault is a working vault. You may see curators working inside it while you admire the carvings.

According to its website, Qaumajuq bridges Canada's North and South and celebrates the North in the South. Indigenous language-keepers named Qaumajuq , which means "it is bright, it is lit." The museum opened in 2021 and connects at every level with the rest of the Winnipeg Art Gallery (WAG) space. The Winnipeg Art Gallery has been collecting Inuit art for decades. It also holds in trust over 7,000 items of the Government of Nunavut's Fine Art Collection.

The first floor of WAG-Qaumajuq is free to visit. You can view Visible Vault carvings at that level without charge. However, it is well worth buying a ticket to view the exhibitions staged in Qaumajuq's gallery spaces. They're likely to challenge any preconceptions you may have about what Inuit art is and impress you with its variety of styles and mediums.

Address 300 Memorial Boulevard, Winnipeg, MB R3C 1V1, +1 (204) 786-6641, www.wag.ca, inquiries@wag.ca | Getting there Bus 16, 18, or 60 to Osborne & York (Stops 10598/10607) or bus 11, 21, 24, or 55 to Portage & Colony (Stop 10545) or Portage & Vaughn (Stop 10580) | Hours Wed–Sun 11am–5pm | Tip Stop by Memorial Park to see its large fountain, inaugurated in 1962, and several military memorials (Memorial Boulevard between Broadway and York Avenues).

81 — Rainbow Resource Centre

The face and heart of the 2SLGBTQ+ community

Rainbow Resource Centre serves Manitoba's lesbian, gay, bisexual, transgender, two spirit, and queer+ communities, providing support and resources for people of all ages, as well as guardians and caregivers. By delivering educational workshops to organizations, schools, and educators to increase awareness of issues, the centre helps to enhance their capacity to serve the community. Materials in the library promote awareness and education as well.

Rainbow is a community centre as well as a resource centre. Drop-in, social support network groups led by volunteers and staff include the popular Crafting Queerly; a group for newcomers to Canada; a support group for parents, family, and friends of trans individuals; and more. Rainbow runs a youth program, a youth summer camp for gender and sexually diverse youth, and an Over The Rainbow group for folks aged 55+.

Notably, Rainbow is North America's longest continuously running 2SLBGTQ+ resource centre. It began in the early 1970s as a University of Manitoba student group known as the Campus Gay Club. Over the years and a number of name and location changes, it became an important resource for the gay and lesbian community. In 1988, it incorporated as a non-profit organization as the Winnipeg Gay/Lesbian Resource Centre. The 1999 name change to Rainbow Resource Centre was done to recognize and be more inclusive of all members of the 2SLGBTQ+ communities.

Rainbow continues to evolve and grow. In 2023, it moved to the historic Wilson House and began to create the Place of Pride campus that would bring housing, community space, and programming together. A new building connected to Wilson House was constructed as Canada's first affordable housing exclusively for 2SLGBTQ+ older adults. It's main floor is a cultural centre. Rainbow continues to nurture inclusive spaces for 2SLGBTQ+ communities to thrive.

Address 545 Broadway Avenue, Winnipeg, MB R3C 0W3, +1 (204) 474-0212, www.rainbowresourcecentre.org, info@rainbowresourcecentre.org | Getting there Bus 10, 17, 20, or 23 to Broadway & Osborne (Stops 10584/10594) or bus 16, 18, or 60 to Osborne & Broadway (Stops 10596/10599) | Hours Mon–Thu 10am–12:30pm & 1:30–5pm; see website for events | Tip Club 200, one of the longest running gay bars in Canada, features a restaurant, karaoke nights, a dance floor, music and entertainment (190 Garry Street, www.club200.ca).

82 Rainbow Stage

Showtunes in an open-air amphitheatre

Taking in a show at Rainbow Stage has been a Winnipeg summer tradition for decades. Rainbow Stage is Canada's leading not-for-profit musical theatre company and Canada's largest and longest-running outdoor theatre. It seats 2,600 people.

Plans for the open-air theatre developed after the 1950 flood damaged Kildonan Park's bandstand. Construction began in 1951 and was completed in time for a September 1953 inaugural concert by the Kitsilano Boys Band from Vancouver. The venue would open officially in July 1954 with a variety benefit concert featuring prominent local artists.

In September 1955 it staged the musical comedy *Brigadoon*, marking the beginning of a tradition. Musical theatre has been a staple here ever since, with productions of many favourite and classic Broadway musicals. Some performances have featured imported stars, but Rainbow Stage mostly employs local directors and actors, including perennial audience favourites. It marked its 70th year in 2024 with the Canadian premiere of the all-Filipino musical *Ma-Buhay!*, which Rainbow Stage commissioned and developed.

A triodetic dome, fabric-covered, aluminum frame roof was added in the early 1970s, and a more rain-proof plastic replaced the fabric a few years later. Other changes in the 1970s included the addition of washrooms, ticket booths, other amenities, and meandering, exposed-concrete walls curving around the auditorium space. A detailed, colourful forest and theatre-themed mural on the outside of those walls was selected as the 2011 Mural of the Year by Murals of Winnipeg.

Although the additions over the years now offer protection from the elements, the venue hasn't lost the feel of an outdoor theatre. Openings between the wall and the roof allow you to feel the outside air and glimpse the trees in the scenic park setting. The park is a lovely spot for a pre-show picnic.

Address 2015 Main Street, Winnipeg, MB R2V 2B9, +1 (204) 989-0888, www.rainbowstage.ca | Getting there Bus 18 or 77 to Main & Kildonan Park (Stops 30023/30024) | Hours Exterior daily 7am–10pm; see website for show hours | Tip Founded in 1925, French-language Théâtre Cercle Molière (340 Provencher Boulevard, www.cerclemoliere.com) is the oldest Canadian theatre company in any language. English subtitles are available.

83 Ralph Connor House
Heritage home of a top-selling Canadian author

The stately Ralph Connor House commands attention even in a neighbourhood where 73 of the 123 homes are historically noteworthy. A circular drive leads to a spacious, three-storey, Jacobean Revival-style home of tapestry-red brick and Tyndall Stone dressings, which has city, provincial, and national heritage designations.

Located on a large riverside lot in Armstrong's Point, a residential area developed for well-to-do families between 1880 and 1920, the house was built in 1913–1914 for Reverend Charles Gordon (1860–1937), a Presbyterian clergyman and top-selling author. Under the pen name Ralph Connor, he wrote numerous novels combining Christian messages with frontier adventures. One of Canada's best-known writers of the time, he lived here with his wife Helen and their seven children until his death.

Since 1939, the house has been home to the University Women's Club of Winnipeg, which unites women for intellectual and social development. Membership is not limited to those with a university background, but also includes anyone concerned about bettering the lives of women and girls around the world. They work for the advancement of education, art, science, literature, and civic reform; promote heritage preservation and improvement of the environment; host educational programs and social events; maintain a Scholarship Trust Fund; and conduct school tours. The club works with the non-profit organization Friends of The Ralph Connor House, who own the building, to preserve the house and its history.

You can request a tour in advance to see the home's interior, which features quarter cut oak woodwork, mahogany paneling, leaded glass, and prominent fireplaces in 23 rooms and 6 bathrooms. Several furniture pieces and décor items from the original owners remain. The space is used for University Women's Club activities and as a rentable event venue.

Address 54 West Gate, Winnipeg, MB R3C 2E1, +1 (204) 954-7880,
www.uwcwpgmb.com, uwc@mymts.net | Getting there Bus 20 or 29 to Maryland &
Misericordia Health Centre (Stop 10815) or bus 20, 29, or 635 to Sherbrook & West Gate
(Stop 10190) | Hours Viewable from the outside only; interior tours by special request |
Tip The 1911 ornamental stone and iron gates at the entrances to the Armstrong's Point
neighbourhood are a Winnipeg Landmark Heritage Structure (East Gate, Middle Gate,
and West Gate at Cornish Avenue, www.mhs.mb.ca/docs/sites/armstrongpointgates.shtml).

84__The REDress Project

Art draws attention to a national crisis

The award-winning design of the Canadian Museum for Human Rights features a limestone base, a curved cloud of glass panes resembling the folded wings of a dove, and a tower rising like a beacon. The building simulates a journey from darkness to light, which is the very experience the museum aims to provide.

The Canadian Journeys gallery here focuses on the steps and missteps towards achieving greater rights in Canada. In one eye-catching exhibit, red dresses appear to float in mid-air. This is the REDress Project permanent art installation, drawing attention to missing and murdered Indigenous women and girls.

A Statistics Canada report stated that between 2009 and 2021, the rate of homicide against First Nations, Métis, and Indigenous women and girls was six times higher than among their non-Indigenous counterparts. Métis artist Jaime Black created the REDress Project as "a visual reminder of the staggering number of women and girls who are no longer with us," as she states on her website. She began in 2010 by gathering hundreds of red dresses to hang in public spaces across Winnipeg and Canada. Red is a powerful colour that represents lifeblood and the connection among all people. It is also a colour the spirits can see.

The REDress Project has been displayed in dozens of places in North America, and the red dress is now the symbol of this crisis. Red Dress Day, a National Day of Awareness for Missing and Murdered Indigenous Women, Girls, and 2-Spirit People is now observed annually on May 5, when people in Canada hang red dresses on trees and porches.

Unique and interactive exhibits in the museum's 10 core galleries across seven floors tell stories of human rights struggles and successes from around the world. Go from floor to floor via stunningly lit alabaster ramps or by elevator. The Israel Asper Tower of Hope at the top offers 360-degree views of Winnipeg.

Address 85 Israel Asper Way, Winnipeg, MB R3C 0L5, +1 (204) 289-2000, www.humanrights.ca, info@humanrights.ca | Getting there Bus 38 to Israel Asper & Canadian Museum for Human Rights (Stops 10901/10902) | Hours Tue–Sun 10am–5pm | Tip Enjoy the 10-minute light show on the Esplanade Riel pedestrian bridge and spire on the hour every hour from sunset to midnight (Provencher Boulevard over the Red River).

85 Residential School Totem Pole

Honouring the children's stories

A 21-metre-tall (69-feet), painted totem pole in Assiniboine Park is dedicated to residential school children. Totem poles are not traditional to Manitoba Indigenous peoples and uncommon around Winnipeg, but the subject of residential schools is deeply felt in Manitoba and across Canada.

The *Story of the Residential School Totem Pole* reflects the personal experience of the artist and other residential school children. Kwakiutl artist Charles Joseph Sr. attended residential school in Alert Bay, British Columbia. He carved the pole in 2015 from a massive, West Coast tree. The totem pole stood for several years in front of the Montreal Museum of Fine Art before coming to Winnipeg as a gift to the Southern Chiefs Organization (SCO). It was unveiled in the park in 2022 and will be moved to the historic Hudson's Bay Building when SCO completes its renovation.

Joseph's website tells the stories of figures carved into the pole, offering pathways to healing from an Indigenous perspective. The Wild Woman of the World takes children back to the ancestors' world. The Whale seeks to provide healing to survivors. Faces around it represent young children adopted or taken from families. The Raven, the trickster, reminds us that survivors are not to be blamed for the pain they endured. White faces represent all the children who never made it home. The Bear spirit will take care of them. The Fox, the storyteller of the north, tells a story to the face of a young boy who helped carve. Kolus at the top of the pole represents Joseph's family. The Sisiulth inside it has supernatural powers. Carved crosses show the crosses Charles carried for many years.

The totem pole is a powerful way to share the residential school stories, honour the children, and seek healing.

Address 2355 Corydon Avenue, Winnipeg, MB, +1 (204) 927-6000, https://www.charlesnativeart.ca/winnipeg assiniboine-park, info@assiniboinepark.ca | Getting there Bus 18 or 79 to Corydon & Shaftesbury (Stops 60471/60472) or 11 or 21 to Portage & Overdale (Stops 20212/20418) | Hours Unrestricted | Tip A totem pole at the St. Vital Park duck pond once stood on the Billinkoff family lumber yard. The Billinkoff family donated it in memory of their father (190 River Road, www.winnipeg.ca).

86   Riel House

1880s Métis home in mourning

A welcoming, two-story, Red River Frame House from 1881 sits on a spacious tree-bordered lawn at Riel House National Historic Site. It was the home of Julie Lagimodière Riel (1820–1906), mother of Louis Riel, whose story is well-known in Manitoba. He led the 1869–1870 Métis resistance to protect Métis land rights and is now regarded as the Father of Manitoba. His father Louis Riel Sr. (1817–1864) was also a champion of Métis rights, and his commitment to the cause undoubtedly influenced his son.

The Riel's original lot stretched from the Red River to the Seine River. The family lived at their mill site along the Seine from the early 1850s until the death of Louis Riel Sr. The younger Louis Riel was studying in Montreal at the time, but Julie and the other children moved to the western end of their land, at first living in a different house than the one you see here today.

Louis Riel never actually lived in the current house, but his body lay in state there for two days in December 1885 following his execution for treason. His wife Marguerite died in the house in the spring of 1886. After that, Louis' mother and his brother Joseph cared for his and Marguerite's two children. Joseph's descendants lived in the house until 1969.

Riel House has been restored to reflect the spring of 1886, when the family was in mourning. During the months of July and August, interpreters provide visitors with information about the house, the family, and their daily life. You'll see a traditional rope bed, as well as examples of Métis beading, and you'll hear about the foods the family ate. The yard provides space for games, music, and Métis cultural events. Riel House provides a look beyond history and politics and into the Riel family's daily lives. The house museum is only open in summer, but you can see the grounds year-round and imagine life under a blanket of snow.

Address 330 River Road, Winnipeg, MB R2M 3Z8, +1 (204) 983-6757, parks.canada.ca/lhn-nhs/mb/riel, manitoba@pc.gc.ca | Getting there Bus 16 to River & Harry Collins (Stops 50458/50691) | Hours July & Aug Fri–Wed 10am–5pm, Thu 1–8pm; Sept–June from the outside only | Tip Visit Louis Riel's grave, marked by a red tombstone surrounded by half-circle stone borders, in the historic St. Boniface Cathedral Cemetery (180 de la Cathédrale Avenue, www.cathedralestboniface.ca).

87__Roblin Centre

Old meets new in striking adaptive design

A group of storefronts dating to the late 1880s form part of the Princess Street wall of Red River College Polytechnic's Roblin Centre. A modern, PV-glass-paned extension stands beside them. Both are part of the Centre's old-meets-new architecture. A former lane is now a bright, three-storey atrium serving as a gathering space and a main corridor through the building. The brick exterior of a former warehouse, including a numbered loading dock door, forms one of the atrium's walls.

Walking down Princess Street, you may find that the restored storefronts are so convincing that you may not realize they are part of the college. Only one of the doors opens into the new building. In that entryway, you'll find floor tiles from one of the former buildings and a pressed tin roof. Step further inside, and you are in a modern space. Open areas, large windows, and exposed ceiling ductwork give it an industrial feel.

Look for the many touches of the past throughout the building. Old radiators stand outside the campus bookstore, which features pieces of original wood and glass. You'll find other pieces of original wood in walkways. On hallway walls, look for installations of hand-painted bank vault doors. Thirty vaults were found when the site was developed. While the section of Main Street known as Banker's Row was the place you'd find many financial institutions during Winnipeg's boom time, many banks and insurance companies rented offices in this block of Princess Street as well in the 1880s.

Located in the Exchange District, a 20-block National Historic Site full of heritage buildings, Roblin Centre's adaptive and sustainable features and historic preservation won many design awards. The building that has preserved pieces of the past now contains state-of-the-art equipment to support students in business and management, creative arts, and information technology.

Address 160 Princess Street, Winnipeg, MB R3B 1K9, www.rrc.ca/edc/roblin-centre | Getting there Bus 12 or 23 to William & Princess (Stops 10721/10722) | Hours Mon–Fri 6am–8pm | Tip Wooden floorboards from the former Winnipeg Roller Rink, a popular hangout for decades, create a distinctive wall in the University of Winnipeg's Richardson College entry atrium (599 Portage Avenue, www.uwinnipeg.ca/richardson-college).

88 Ross House Museum

The first post office in Western Canada

Ross House was built in 1854 for William and Jemima Ross, members of a prominent Scottish Métis family. Their house became Western Canada's first official post office when William Ross was appointed Postmaster in 1855 and operated the office out of his home. Prior to that, the only way to get mail to and from the area had been through the Hudson's Bay Company or the Northwest Company.

The Ross House Museum showcases the history of the Ross Family and the early postal service in Western Canada. The postmaster's desk, postal weights, and letters are among original artifacts on display at the Ross House Museum. Period furnishings include family items, such as wooden chests, and a spinning wheel. Sitting on a shelf in this Presbyterian family's home, an intriguing game box disguised to look like a book would have fooled their visitors. Now well-worn, the "book" opened up for a game of checkers on the outside and backgammon on the inside. Six Red River chairs and an embroidered caribou tie for a child are just some of the interesting objects you'll find in the house.

William Ross died of tuberculosis in 1856. In order to support her young family, Jemima leased and sold sections of the land left to the children. Much of Winnipeg's north Exchange District was built on the Ross River lot. In 1875, Jemima donated land to the city for its first market. The house, which has been moved twice before winding up in its current Point Douglas location, retains the original wooden floor planking.

The weathered grey colour of the house's exterior wood seems fitting for Winnipeg's second oldest house, which was built using the Red River Frame construction method. The interior is open to visitors only during summer months, but you can visit the grounds of the site any time of the year and read the family's stories on the stone markers in front of the house.

Address 140 Meade Street North, Winnipeg, MB, +1 (204) 942-5396, www.sevenoakshouse.ca, rhousemuseum@gmail.com | Getting there Bus 45 to Euclid & Argyle (Stops 30434/30545) | Hours Exterior unrestricted; Interior June–Aug Wed–Sat 10am–4pm | Tip Markian Shashkevich Park next to Ross House hosts monuments to Ukrainian settlers, Ukrainian-Canadian veterans from World War II, and the park's poet namesake, who was Ukrainian (164 Hallet Street, parkmaps.winnipeg.ca).

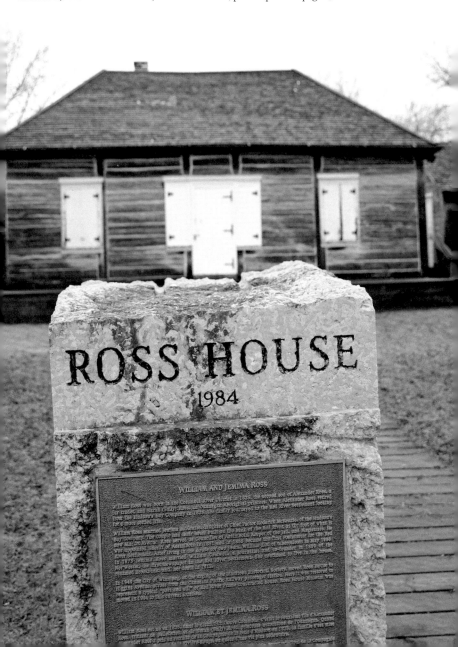

89 Rotary Heritage Park

First steam locomotive built in Western Canada

A restored, 1926 steam locomotive rests inside a shelter at Transcona's Rotary Heritage Park. The shelter's roof and solid back wall protect the engine from the elements, while metal fencing on the other three sides allows for public viewing. The numbers 2747 appear in red on the side of the black locomotive.

Transcona developed in the early 1900s after the Grand Trunk Railway, predecessor of the Canadian National Railway, purchased land for a railway repair and maintenance shop and a townsite. The town incorporated in 1912, and Transcona Shops opened in 1913. Transcona received city status in 1961. It became part of Winnipeg in the 1972 amalgamation of the city with surrounding municipalities. The railway remains a significant employer in the community. Between 1926 and 1931, Transcona Shops built an estimated 33 steam locomotives for the Canadian National Railway. CN 2747, a Consolidation model considered to be the ultimate heavy-freight locomotive of the day, was the first. Its construction took 27 days. It was used mainly as a freight hauler and began operations in Alberta. As a side note, during both world wars, Transcona Shops secretly manufactured munitions, as well as an armoured train for the Canadian Army in 1941.

In 1955, the Canadian government arranged for CN 2747 to pull troop trains from Wabowden to Churchill in northern Manitoba. Later, in 1957, it worked in The Pas, Manitoba. By 1960, the steam era had ended, and hundreds of retired steam locomotives awaited demolition at Transcona Rail Yards. This locomotive was the only one to survive and was placed on permanent outdoor display in what was then Kiwanis Park. The Transcona Museum acquired it in 2015, and it underwent preservation work in 2018 to 2020 to ensure its stability and longevity after 60 years of damage from the elements, vandalism, and theft. The protective enclosure was completed in 2023.

Address 735 Kildare Avenue West, Winnipeg, MB, parkmaps.winnipeg.ca | Getting there Bus 47 or 89 to Kildare & Kootenay (Stops 40113/40114) | Hours Unrestricted | Tip The Transcona Museum shares the history of Transcona and its railway roots with three galleries of exhibits that change on a yearly basis (141 Regent Avenue West, www.transconamuseum.mb.ca).

90 Royal Canadian Mint

Making coins for Canada and the world

Dozens of flags line the drive leading to the Royal Canadian Mint, a dramatic, triangular-shaped building rising up like a mountain. Designed by Manitoba architect Étienne Gaboury, the Winnipeg Mint opened in 1976. It produces all of the Canadian coins in circulation, as well as circulation coins for countries around the world. The flags along the drive represent the countries for which this mint has created coins. The building sits on beautifully landscaped grounds bordering a man-made lake.

Inside, glass walls along one side of the lobby offer a view into the packaging and mailing area, but to see the rest of the minting process, you need to go to the second floor on one of the Mint's guided tours. Display cases contain collections of foreign and Canadian coins through the years. A corridor with large windows goes past the production areas. Guides walk you through the processes and tell you about the state-of-the-art equipment. You'll learn about the skill that goes into designing a coin and how that design gets onto the coins that might eventually wind up in your pocket.

As the guides explain the process, they share information about major milestones and unique stories, such as the one about the coin that became known as the "spy coin." In 2004, the Royal Canadian Mint issued the 25-cent Canadian poppy coin, the world's first coloured circulation coin. The red inlaid image and fluorescent coating made a couple of US defense contractors so suspicious they filed an espionage report about the coin.

When you return to the main floor, take time to browse through the attractive boutique and assorted displays. See the unique 2010 Vancouver Winter Olympic and Paralympic medals. You can even strike your own token. Note that Canada has two Royal Canadian Mints. The other one is in Ottawa and produces collector coins, gold and silver bullion, and medals and medallions.

Address 520 Lagimodière Boulevard, Winnipeg, MB R2J 3E7, +1 (204) 984-1144, www.mint.ca | Getting there By car, take Lagimodière Boulevard to south of Fermor Avenue and north of Abinojii Mikanah | Hours See website for seasonal hours | Tip Precious Blood Roman Catholic Church, also designed by Étienne Gaboury, features curving brick walls and spiraling, cedar-shake roof to resemble a tipi (200 Kenny Street, www.paroisseduprecieuxsang.ca).

91 __ Selkirk Avenue Bell Tower

Meeting place with history and purpose

A bell tower stands on the north side of Selkirk Avenue in Selkirk Square. Its onion dome top resembles the domes on nearby Ukrainian churches. Its bronze bell dates to 1877.

The bronze bell hung in Winnipeg's original market building near Main Street and William Avenue, where it was rung at specific times or to summon the fire department. When the market was rebuilt in 1889, the bell was moved to the tower on the "gingerbread" City Hall. That building was demolished in the early 1960s, and the bell was put into storage at the Museum of Man and Nature, now called the Manitoba Museum. The bell rang again on June 21, 1985 after being removed from storage and installed in the Selkirk Avenue Bell Tower.

In the early 1900s, Selkirk Avenue was the commercial hub of the city's early Jewish and Eastern European communities. In recent decades, it's become a focal point for the urban Indigenous population. Selkirk Square was created in the 1980s as part of a Core Area Initiative to improve the historic neighbourhood, which had experienced a period of decline. Powers Street was closed off north and south of Selkirk Avenue to create a pedestrian plaza with seating areas and murals on the sides of adjacent buildings. The bell tower was erected as a landmark and a meeting place.

Today, the bell rings regularly on Friday evenings to announce "Meet Me at the Bell Tower" events. Indigenous youth-led meetings, which occur on the first and third Fridays of the month in the next-door Indigenous Family Centre, are a chance to meet neighbours and build a stronger community. Each week's meeting focuses on a different theme important to the community. "Meet Me at the Bell Tower" began in 2011, initiated by the Aboriginal Youth Opportunities organization with a focus on bringing people together to demand an end to violence. The bell tower has been bringing people together ever since.

Address Selkirk Avenue at Powers Street, Winnipeg, MB | **Getting there** Bus 16 or 97 to Selkirk & Salter West (Stops 30196/30198) | **Hours** Unrestricted | **Tip** Gunn's Bakery has been providing customers with old country, kosher baking since 1937 (247 Selkirk Avenue, www.gunnsbakery.com).

92 Seven Oaks House Museum

Oldest and maybe most haunted house in Winnipeg

Seven Oaks House Museum is the oldest surviving residence in Winnipeg. It may also be the most haunted. The house was built in 1851–1853 for John Inkster (1799–1874), a farmer, merchant, and free-trader, and his wife Mary (1804–1892). They had 11 children, 9 of whom lived to adulthood. Many original Inkster belongings, such as furniture made by John, and the family's china, photographs, and beadwork, give the museum a personal and authentic feel. The parlour, filled with fine furnishings and of a size equal to an entire house for many other families, reflects the well-to-do status of the influential Scottish Métis family.

Each room holds many stories – and perhaps lingering spirits. In his book *Haunted Winnipeg* and on his walking tours with Winnipeg Ghost Walk, Matthew Komus recounts paranormal events within the house. You may or may not sense a mysterious presence yourself, but museum staff have heard footsteps and loud, smashing sounds when the house is otherwise empty. They've found toys and dolls re-arranged in the children's room. Non-working clocks have started to tick again. The dining room, where the Inskster's son-in-law William McMurray died in 1877 when he choked at the dinner table, is reportedly one of the more active rooms. Visitors have fled the second-floor master bedroom, complaining of headaches and nausea. Mary suffered from migraines and often rested on the room's chaise lounge.

For something eerie but not necessarily haunted, look for the framed works of human hair art, the upholstered chair decorated with bison horns, and the child's rocking horse covered in real horse hide.

The home is open May through August, and you can explore the exterior and access the surrounding park year-round. Look for commemorative plaques, a heritage garden, and more outdoor displays.

Address 50 Mac Street, Winnipeg, MB R2V 4Z9, +1 (204) 339-7429, www.sevenoakshouse.ca, SOHMuseum@gmail.com | Getting there Bus 18 to Main & Rupertsland (Stops 30045/30046) | Hours Park: Daily 7am–10pm; Museum: May–Aug Wed–Sat 10am–4pm | Tip Seven Oaks Monument, the oldest historic marker in Western Canada, commemorates the 1816 Battle of Seven Oaks between fur trade rivals, the Hudson's Bay Company and the North West Company, during the Pemmican War (northeast corner of Main Street and Rupertsland Boulevard).

93 Snow Maze
Officially the largest in the world

If you visit A Maze in Corn from August to October, you'll find a corn maze, petting zoo, a bale pyramid, and hayrides. But if you visit in the winter, you'll find a giant snow maze.

In 2019, the Masse family created a 2,789-square-metre (30,000-square-foot) maze created from snow. It earned *The Guinness Book of World Records* title for the World's Largest Snow Maze. The Masse family kept expanding the maze in subsequent years until it almost doubled in size. They enhanced it with snow sculptures, snow art, and themed "rooms." At the site, they added a snow mountain with tobogganing, a luge run, sleigh rides, snow games, and warming areas with bonfires. Snow buildings house a snow bar, live entertainment, and a restaurant. Look for snow art in every building.

Each year's maze design is different, and the designs in the five themed rooms change as well. Examples of past themes include "Alice in Wonderland" and "Pigs in Space." It takes 20 people, 10 artists, two months, and sophisticated equipment to construct the maze. Snow guns create artificial snow that is packed into forms to create the walls in much the same way as concrete for a basement. The walls stand nearly two metres (6.5 feet) tall.

The Snow Maze is typically open from early to mid-January through mid-March, but exact dates vary from year to year depending on the weather. The length of time to make it through the maze depends on how quickly you find the key pathways and how much time you linger to admire the artwork. Clint Masse says it typically takes 45 minutes, give or take 20.

Whether you visit in the afternoon or the evening when the lights come on, the Snow Maze provides a fun way for the whole family to celebrate winter. Adults say that navigating the maze makes them feel like kids again. Enjoy hot cocoa or an adult beverage afterwards, and take in the other on-site activities.

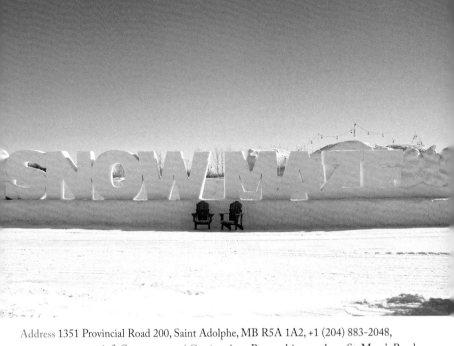

Address 1351 Provincial Road 200, Saint Adolphe, MB R5A 1A2, +1 (204) 883-2048, www.cornmaze.ca, info@cornmaze.ca | Getting there By car, drive south on St. Mary's Road (Provincial Road 200) | Hours See website | Tip For more winter fun, skate the Nestaweya River Trail in the heart of downtown and see design award-winning warming huts (1 Forks Market Road, www.theforks.com).

94 Sous Sol

Candlelit dinner and drinks in the basement

Sous Sol is literally a hidden gem – there is no signage to identify the presence of this cozy French restaurant. Lettering on the door says *Vandelay Industries*, a reference to a fictional company George Costanza made up on *Seinfeld* to extend his unemployment benefits. Stairs on the other side of that door take you down into a dim, candlelit basement room.

"Sous sol" is French for basement.

The vibe here is both fun and sophisticated. A brick wall with a wide archway in the middle divides the lounge area from the dining room. There is an eclectic collection of antique tables and chairs, and old paintings hang on the walls. Hardened drips of wax coat a candelabra hanging above a serving table in the middle of the dining area.

The concise menu, which changes every three to four weeks, allows for a focus on quality. You may find oysters, beef tartare, and roast bone marrow, followed by MB beef tenderloin or grilled boar chops with potatoes dauphinoise or spaetzle in wild mushroom sauce, with crème brûlée for dessert. Ingredients are ethically sourced from small, local farms, and the food is served on mismatched china collected from thrift shops to enjoy a place of honour once again on your table. The cocktail menu features original recipes, flaming cocktails, and a selection of low alcohol and zero-proof drinks. The cocktail menu also changes over time, but not as frequently as the food menu. Reservations are recommended, although walk-ups are accepted if there is room. You'll also find a late-night menu and happy hour drinks after 10:30 pm.

You may have to use the flashlight on your phone to read the menu options in the dim light, but put it away after that so you can soak up the atmosphere. You can forget about the outside world and feel transported to another place and time as you enjoy a romantic evening or time with friends over excellent food.

Address 22-222 Osborne Street, Winnipeg, MB R3L 1Z3, www.soussolosborne.com, monsieur@soussolosborne.com | Getting there Bus 16, 18, or 60 to Osborne & Osborne Junction (Stops 10066/10067/10068) | Hours Wed & Thu 5pm–midnight, Fri & Sat 5pm–1am | Tip Take a cocktail-making class at Patent 5 Distillery, a craft distillery operating out of a former livery stable in the historic Exchange District (108 Alexander Avenue, www.patent5.ca).

95 St. Boniface Heritage Garden

A monument to the Catholic sisters of Manitoba

An eye-catching bronze and stainless-steel sculpture sits in the St. Boniface Heritage Garden at the residence of the Archbishop of St. Boniface. Titled *Spiritu Vocat* in Latin, *Appel de l'esprit* in French, and *Spirit's Call* in English, the 2016 sculpture by Madeleine Vrignon celebrates the work of Catholic sisters instrumental in developing Manitoba's health, education, and social service systems. The three languages speak to the sisters' chronological history since 1844, when religious women first arrived in St. Boniface.

Vrignon says the sculpture can be viewed through a lens of interwoven metaphors. The apex, supported by two stainless-steel bands, draws our gaze upward to an imagined horn beckoning women into service. From the side, the metal shape evokes the prow of a canoe that brought the first Grey nuns from Québec. Diagonal supports rhythmically paddle forward. From within, we are welcomed into a created space where a dynamic unfolds. A kneeling nun in traditional habit turns her face upward in gratitude and acknowledgement, accepting her mission. Her outstretched hand reaches across to a second nun, a postulant in a modernized, 1960s'-era habit, and invites future women into service. Long metal bands, like a *ceinture fléchée*, or Métis sash, extend and anchor us firmly in Manitoba. Woven from the centre outwards, the sash represents women's religious groups, who have woven the fabric of society through service to hospitals, schools, orphanages, and other social services.

Sit and reflect on a bench, and read the interpretive panels about the work of these pioneering women. The sculpture evokes a peaceful feeling, as does the entire garden, where you'll also find a fountain, a dedication to the Oblates of Mary Immaculate, and a tribute to the Métis Nation.

Address 151 de la Cathédrale Avenue, Winnipeg, MB R2H 0H6, +1 (204) 237-9851, www.archsaintboniface.ca, reception@archsaintboniface.ca | Getting there Bus 10 or 43 to Provencher & Taché (Stops 50176/50177) | Hours Unrestricted | Tip La Maison des artistes visuels francophones has a sculpture garden with permanent sculptures and ephemeral projects in a beautiful green space (219 Provencher Boulevard, www.maisondesartistes.mb.ca/autour-de-la-maison).

96 — St. John's Cemetery
19th-century crowd funding

In St. John's Anglican Cemetery, shaded by mature trees around a central, Gothic-style cathedral, tombstones mark the resting places of many of Winnipeg's founding families and Manitoba's prominent historical figures. One of the tallest and grandest monuments is the result of a nineteenth-century version of crowdfunding.

Made mostly of native limestone, the monument to John Norquay stands at the western end of the cemetery. Above the base where his name is engraved, polished granite pillars support an arch with the provincial coat of arms. A plaque sits between the pillars. A five-metre (17-foot), red, polished granite column capped with a cross of native stone towers above.

Of Scottish and Indigenous descent, John Norquay (1941–1889) was Manitoba's Premier from 1878 to 1887. Until Louis Riel was given the honorary title of First Premier of Manitoba in 2023, Norquay was considered the first Premier of Indigenous origin. Along with Louis Riel, he played an instrumental role in attaining provincial status for Manitoba. His government fell in 1877 because of questionable financial transactions with the Hudson's Bay Railway, but he was re-elected the following year and became Leader of the Opposition.

His family had very little money when he died suddenly in 1889. But he had been well regarded, and a committee formed to raise money to build a monument for him, with a maximum donation limit of $1 per person to give all classes in the community an opportunity to contribute. The monument by sculptor Samuel Hooper (1851–1911) was unveiled on August 1, 1891. Words on the plaque read, *This monument is a public expression of his worth.*

Founded in 1820, St. John's is the oldest Anglican parish west of the Great Lakes. Wander through the rest of the cemetery to see many other memorials and monuments, as well as a 1659 bronze and copper sundial.

IN THE MEMORY OF
THE HON. JOHN NORQUAY
WHO WAS FOR MANY YEARS
PREMIER OF MANITOBA
BY HIS SUDDEN AND ALL TOO EARLY DEATH
HIS NATIVE LAND LOST AN ELOQUENT SPEAKER
AN HONEST STATESMAN AND A TRUE FRIEND
BORN MAY 8TH 1841
DIED JULY 5 1889
THIS MONUMENT IS A PUBLIC EXPRESSION
OF HIS STERLING WORTH.

NORQUAY

Address 135 Anderson Avenue, Winnipeg, MB R2W 5M9, +1 (204) 586-8385,
www.stjohnscathedral.ca | Getting there Bus 18 to Main & Anderson (Stop 30075) or
Main & Church (Stops 30073/20074) | Hours Mon–Sat 9am–4pm, Sun 8am–4pm |
Tip In St. John's Park, the Kapabamayak Achaak Healing Forest, a gathering place based
on the Medicine Wheel, provides space for quiet reflection and ceremony (1 Fowler
Street, www.healingforestwpg.org).

97__ St. Norbert Chapel
Worshiping in an open-air chapel

Tucked away at the end of a residential street across from the St. Norbert Parish church is the open-air chapel of Chapelle de Notre-Dame-du-Bon-Secours, also known as The Chapel of Our Lady of Good Help, or St. Norbert Chapel. The white building with blue trim has a gabled roof and horizontal wood siding on its three outside walls. This chapel, now a Provincial Heritage Site, is one of the few remaining open-air religious structures that once dotted the province.

Father Noël-Joseph Ritchot (1825–1905) and his parishioners began construction of the chapel in 1870. It is dedicated to the Virgin Mary, whom Ritchot credited with interceding in the 1869–1870 dispute between the Métis Nation and the Canadian Government. That conflict ended with the negotiation to add Métis land, language, and school rights into the Manitoba Act, which created the province of Manitoba.

An open east wall provides a view into the small, peaceful sanctuary, but a decorative iron gate blocks physical access inside, except on summer weekends when the gate is opened for visitors. A centre aisle bordered by a handful of plain wooden pews on either side leads to a raised, elaborate, white and blue altar. A statue of the Virgin Mary stands in a niche above the altar. Dark wooden wainscotting covers the lower part of the stucco walls, and arched windows on the side walls let in the light. The painted scenes on the panelled ceiling are replicas, created by artist Robert Freynet, of original murals painted by Constantin Tauffenbach (1829–1890) in the mid-1880s. Those paintings deteriorated over time and are now stored in the St. Norbert Parish church, which maintains the outdoor chapel.

The chapel, which is both simple and ornate, remains a historical and spiritual landmark. Situated among mature trees at the corner of quiet streets, it evokes a feeling of serenity and reverence.

Address 80 St. Pierre Street, Winnipeg, MB R3V 1J8, +1 (204) 269-3240, www.stnorbertparish.ca, paroissestnorbcrt@gmail.com | **Getting there** Bus 91 to De L'Église & St. Pierre (Stop 60753) | **Hours** Exterior unrestricted; Chapel gates open May–Oct Sat & Sun & first Fri 9am–dusk | **Tip** The oldest log church still in regular use in Western Canada is located in the historic St. James Cemetery and holds services in July and August (525 Tylehurst Street, www.stjamesanglicanchurch.ca).

98 St. Norbert Provincial Heritage Park

Luxury living back in the day

You may have glimpsed St. Norbert Provincial Heritage Park while driving south out of the city. If you've never stopped to visit, you might want to change that. The park sits at the junction of the Red and LaSalle Rivers, sometimes called Winnipeg's "other forks." In addition to riverside trails and picnic areas, the peaceful space hosts heritage homes moved from their original locations to recreate Franco-Manitoban life in the late 1800s and early 1900s.

The shells of Delorme House and Henderson House, examples of early Red River Frame architecture, sit unrestored behind a chain-link fence. But two other homes have been restored. The comfortable Turenne House reflects a typical middle-class home. The larger, more elegant Bohémier House features a gambrel roof, not common to the area – its style was imported from Québec. A small building beside the house appears to be a large outhouse, but it is actually an outdoor refrigerator. A block of ice loaded into the loft kept items on the main level cool until after the spring thaw. Although outdoor refrigerators would have been common at one time, very few remain intact.

Wander through the pretty grounds, look at the building exteriors, and read the signage. You can join interior tours of Turenne House and Bohémier House at select times during summer months. Look for beautiful woodwork throughout Bohémier House. Replicas of the original wallpaper, recreated from a sample found during restoration, cover the walls. But the second-floor, indoor outhouse was truly something special. Vented to the outside to keep smells out of the house, the two-seater toilet would have been a lovely luxury on the coldest of winter days. The pots needed to be emptied daily. That job fell to the youngest daughter.

Address 40 Turnbull Drive, Winnipeg, MB R3V 1X2, +1 (204) 945-7273, www.gov.mb.ca/sd/parks/park-maps-and-locations/central/norbert.html, parks@gov.mb.ca | Getting there By car, drive south on Pembina Highway/Highway 75, turn east on Turnbull Drive. | Hours Park open daily 8am–11pm; see website for tour schedule | Tip La Barrière Monument marks the spot of an 1869 Métis blockade that forced negotiations leading to Manitoba becoming a province (west side of Pembina Highway at south end of St. Norbert Bridge).

99 — St. Vital Museum

The Guess Who's gold records

St. Vital was its own city before the 1972 amalgamation of Winnipeg with surrounding municipalities. The St. Vital Museum, located inside a former fire and police station, showcases the community's history from its beginnings in the early 1800s through to the present day. It may surprise you to find a famous rock band's gold records in this community museum.

The Guess Who from Winnipeg achieved international success in the late 1960s and early 1970s with such chart-topping hits as "These Eyes," "Laughing," and "American Woman." The band's exhibit here contains the gold and platinum records and Gold Leaf awards presented to Jim Kale, the band's original bassist, who grew up in St. Vital. The band's original name was Chad Allen and the Expressions, and the other members were Bob Ashley, Randy Bachman, and Garry Peterson. The exhibit shares photos from those early days, as well as the record "Shakin' All Over." As a publicity ploy, the band sent their 1965 cover of this Johnny Kidd song to radio stations with the band name listed as "Guess Who?" The name stuck.

Burton Cummings replaced Ashley in 1965. A few months later Allen left the band, and Cummings became sole lead singer. Bachman quit the band in 1970. Cummings led the band with some line-up changes until 1975, when he disbanded the group. Band members reunited at times, including a performance at the closing ceremony at the Winnipeg 1999 Pan-American Games. The band was inducted into the Canadian Music Hall of Fame in 1987.

You'll also find a Garnet amplifier in the display. The Guess Who used Garnet amps exclusively. They were produced in Winnipeg by Thomas Garnet Gillies, which closed in 1989, but the amps are still valued for their durability and unique sound. Among the other displays at the museum, look for items highlighting the career of *My Big Fat Greek Wedding* actress and Winnipeg native Nia Vardalos.

Address 600 St. Mary's Road, Winnipeg, MB R2M 3L5, +1 (204) 255-2864, www.svhs.ca, info@svhs.ca | Getting there Bus 14 to St. Mary's & St. Anne's (Stops 50285/50286) or bus 55 to St. Anne's & Blenheim (Stop 50550) or St. Anne's & St. Mary's (Stop 50284) | Hours See website for seasonal hours and tours | Tip The tribute *Mural to the Guess Who*, painted by Michael Bridgford-Read, Marymound youth, and St. John's High School students, is a collage of the band's album covers (1400 Main Street).

100_ Stonewall Quarry Park

Leisure time in a former limestone quarry

Amid its natural areas, Stonewall Quarry Park retains remnants of the limestone quarries that once existed on the site. Walking trails wind around a beautiful pond and fountain, through trees and shrubs, and past rock formations. Along the way, you'll find quarry ruins and interpretive signage.

Quarrying in the area began in the 1880s and led to the creation of the town of Stonewall. At first, the quarries mined ordinary building stone. A number of notable limestone buildings still line Main Street. However, it was the high-quality quicklime produced in kilns by burning limestone that the quarries became known for. The whiteness of this product placed it in high demand. A group of original pot kilns can be found along the trail. Big draw kilns with larger capacity replaced pot kilns in 1900, and some of them tower prominently in the park. Fences surround the crumbling structures for safety reasons, but the kilns remain an impressive sight with the tops visible from most spots within the park. A multi-year restoration project will ensure the kilns stand as a reminder of the town's history for years to come.

Also check out the Red Pit of Doom, a former test pit. The rusty colour you see indicates the presence of iron, which was disastrous for a quarry. When you put limestone and iron together into a kiln, they explode.

Interactive exhibits at the Interpretive Centre, open during the summer, engage all ages. Find out about Ordovician Period fossils, the creation of limestone, Manitoba's rock layers, quarry trade secrets, and the families who owned the original quarries. Use the simulator to see how well you can drive a large wheel loader. Discover the many uses for limestone, including in your toothpaste.

Quarrying ended in Stonewall in 1968, but its importance in the town's history is remembered in this pretty park at the north end of Main Street.

Address 166 Main Street, Stonewall, MB R0C 2Z0, +1 (204) 467-7980, www.stonewallquarrypark.ca, stoneqp@stonewall.ca | Getting there By car, drive north on Highway 7, turn west onto Highway 67 to Stonewall, turn north onto Main Street | Hours Park and trails: unrestricted; Interpretive Centre: May–Aug daily 11am–5pm | Tip Stop for lunch at McLeod House, located in a historic home dating to the early 1900s. Book ahead for high tea (Stonewall, www.mcleodhousetearoom.com).

101 __ Sturgeon Creek Fishway

Observation deck atop a fish ladder

The sights and sounds from the observation deck atop the fish ladder on the west side of Sturgeon Creek invite you to linger. The low hum of traffic from nearby Portage Avenue fades into the background as you listen to burbling water and singing birds and look out over the creek, the greenway beside it, and the grist mill on the other side.

Grant's Old Mill is a working replica of a mill built by Cuthbert Grant on Sturgeon Creek in 1891 to feed his Métis people. It is believed to be the first water-powered mill west of the Great Lakes. The exact location of that original mill is not known, as Grant abandoned the mill after about three years because the dam washed out in successive spring floods. The ribbon-cutting ceremony for the replica mill occurred in 1975. It is now open to visitors during summer months.

More than 30 streams and creeks once flowed through what is now Winnipeg. Sturgeon Creek is the largest of the few remaining streams. It was once a valuable spawning and rearing area for a number of fish species, but urbanization and agriculture had taken a toll by the 1990s. The first steps of a watershed rehabilitation project, initiated in 1993, created four riffle structures in the lower reaches to provide pools of deeper water for spawning. Later riffle structures were added at Grant's Old Mill. In 2001, the fish ladder was built to allow fish passage upstream. When the original mill was built, a dam had been created so that water flowing through it would turn the water wheel. The vertical, cement ladder acts as a trough enabling fish to get around the dam.

Signage at the entrance to the observation deck provides information on some of the over 30 species of fish in Sturgeon Creek. Not only does the fish ladder provide access for fish to more feeding, spawning, and wintering habitats, its observation deck offers humans a pretty, peaceful view.

Address Sturgeon Creek Parkway, north of Portage Avenue on the west side of Sturgeon Creek | Getting there Bus 11 or 21 to Portage & Sturgeon (Stops 20230/20262), take pathway north of Portage Avenue and east of Sturgeon Road | Hours Unrestricted | Tip View St. Andrews Lock and Dam, which also has a fish ladder, from Lockport Provincial Heritage Park. It's the only lock on the prairies and the only surviving moveable dam of its type in the world (Lockport, MB, www.gov.mb.ca/sd/parks/park-maps-and-locations/central/lockport.htmls).

102 Times Change(d) High & Lonesome Club

Winnipeg's favourite honky-tonk

John Scoles began hanging out at blues bar Times Change after returning to Winnipeg in 1992. When he took over the club, he retained the name to remember its legacy and also added to it as he put his own, somewhat quirky stamp on the bar. Now called Times Change(d) High & Lonesome Club, the bar has been a popular hangout for music lovers and a favourite stage for musicians for decades. It won a 2022 Western Canadian Music Award for Impact in Live Music.

A small stage in a not-very-large room creates a connection between musicians and audience. Bands just starting out, big-time musicians, and JUNO-award winners have played on that stage. Roots and blues music are its foundation, but Scoles features the local wealth of musical talent and also brings in musicians from other places. Sunday night blues jam with the legendary Big Dave McLean, who received the Order of Canada in 2019, is the longest-running blues jam in the country.

A 2019 restoration of the 1882 Fortune Building housing the bar by businessman John Pollard gave the bar more space, but Scoles retained its rustic decor. Inspired by bars in the American South, he calls the style "Ramshackle Grandeur." Plain tables with an assortment of chairs and stools sit on a wood plank floor, and their placement encourages socializing. Layers of posters, signs, and other objects on the walls form a living scrapbook. A welcoming vibe draws an eclectic crowd of people of all walks of life.

Scoles, a musician himself, wants people to feel Times Change(d) High and Lonesome Club is a home away from home. He'd like you to feel good about yourself, believe in yourself, and believe that anything is possible. As you connect with great music and friendly people in this off-beat space, you cannot help but feel good.

Address 234 Main Street, Winnipeg, MB R3C 1A8, +1 (204) 957-0982, www.highandlonesomeclub.ca, info@highandlonesomeclub.ca | Getting there Bus 14, 19, 47, or 55 to Main & St. Mary (Stops 10639/11051) or St. Mary & Fort (Stop 10620) or BLUE to Main & St. Mary (Stop 10639) or Main & Broadway (Stop 10625) | Hours See website for events schedule | Tip Pop in for breakfast or lunch at Modern Electric Lunch, inspired by Electric Lunch No. 2, Winnipeg's first restaurant with an electric refrigerator (232 Main Street, www.melunch.ca).

103 Trappist Monastery Park
Our Lady of the Prairie monastery ruins

The brick-and-stone remnants of a former monastery sit among mature trees in a tranquil setting alongside the La Salle River in a south Winnipeg suburb. Monks of the Order of Cistercians of the Strict Observance, known as Trappists, once lived in what is now a provincial park. The shell of their Romanesque-Revival church, built in 1903–1904, stands in the centre of the park, its western façade remains largely intact. The foundation of the residential wing lays perpendicular to the church.

Trappist monks from the Abbey of Bellefontaine in France established the monastery in 1892 upon invitation by Monsignor Noël-Joseph Ritchot (1825–1905), priest of St. Norbert parish, and Archbishop Alexandre-Antonin Taché (1823–1894) of St. Boniface. Named Our Lady of the Prairies, the self-sustaining monastery included milking barns, stables, a cheese house, apiary, sawmill, and cannery. The monks lived a quiet life of prayer, work, and contemplation. But they'd move to a new site near Holland, Manitoba as urban encroachment threatened their peaceful solitude. In 2020, with only two monks left, that property was put up for sale.

In 1983, five years after the monks vacated the monastery along the La Salle River, fire gutted the church and residential wing. The stabilized ruins and surrounding grounds now form Trappist Monastery Provincial Heritage Park. Every spring, Shakespeare in the Ruins stages theatre performances here in the park. At the edge of the property, a former guesthouse, which escaped the fire, houses the St. Norbert Arts Centre. Look for the World Peace Pagoda behind the Arts Centre and overlooking the river. It was constructed in 2000 by the Dharma Centre of Winnipeg and the Buddhist community of Manitoba.

The city's expansion may have crept too close for the monks' comfort, but the park still has a secluded feel to it.

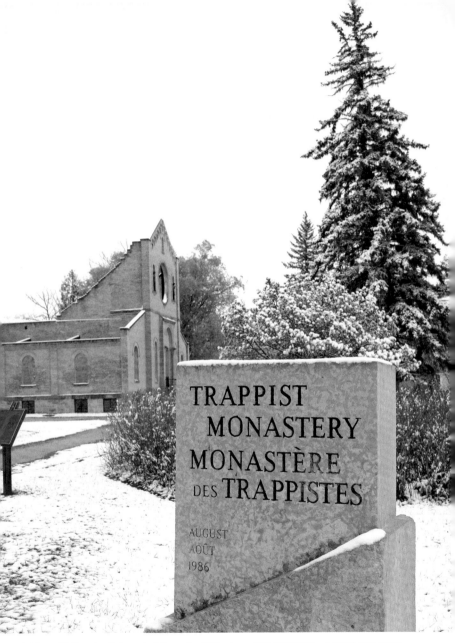

TRAPPIST
MONASTERY
MONASTÈRE
DES TRAPPISTES

AUGUST
AOÛT
1986

Address 80 Rue des Ruines du Monastère, Winnipeg, MB R3V 0B1, +1 (204) 945-7273, www.gov.mb.ca/sd/parks, parks@gov.mb.ca | Getting there By car, drive on Pembina Highway (Highway 75) south of the Perimeter Highway to just before the St. Norbert Bridge, turn west on Rue des Trappistes to Rue des Ruines du Monastère | Hours Unrestricted | Tip La Barrière Park contains a beachfront canoe and kayak launch for paddling on the La Salle River (4403 Waverley Road, RM of Richot, www.winnipeg.ca).

104 Tribute to Manitoba Music Museum

A classic diner with Manitoba music history

There's more than burgers and all-day breakfasts waiting for you at Salisbury House's Pembina Highway location. Within display cases along two walls of the lobby is the "Tribute to Manitoba Music Museum," a look into Manitoba's musical past.

Look for gold records, posters, photographs, information about musicians from Manitoba, and instruments once owned by Manitoba musical icons. A guitar featuring the National Hockey League logo bears the signatures of hockey superstar Bobby Hull (1939–2023) and legendary rock-and-roller Neil Young. Rock musician Burton Cummings, known for his time with The Guess Who and for his solo career, composed songs on the 1891 Heinzman piano here. A working, 1948 Rock-Ola jukebox figures prominently. David C. Rockola (1897–1993), originally from Virden, Manitoba, founded the Rock-Ola company to make coin-operated pinball games and gumball machines. The switch to jukeboxes seems fitting for someone with his surname.

This Salisbury House location and the music museum opened in 2012. It was the vision of Earl Barish, then President and CEO of Salisbury House, and his wife Cheryl. They'd collected many of the pieces, including Cummings' Heinzman piano, at charity events and auctions. And some of the featured musicians have a personal connection with the diner. Neil Young hung out at the previous Pembina Highway location. The Guess Who would visit the Main Street Salisbury House after gigs.

Sals, as the chain is commonly referred to, had its start in Winnipeg when Ralph Erwin opened a tiny, all-night café serving the latest craze from the United States: the hamburger. He called his version of the hamburger a "nip." The nip, made with Manitoba beef, a fresh-baked bun, and grilled onions, remains a mainstay of the menu.

Address 759 Pembina Highway, Winnipeg, MB R3M 2L9, +1 (204) 453-6404, www.salisburyhouse.ca/locations | Getting there Bus 60 to Pembina & Stafford (Stops 10085/10086) | Hours Daily 6am–11pm | Tip A cairn in Pembina Highway's median strip (Pembina Highway at Stafford Street) marks the northern end of the Pine to Palm Highway, a route between Winnipeg and New Orleans, Louisiana.

105 __ Ukrainian Museum

One stitch tells a thousand stories

Topped with onion domes and decorated with a Holy Trinity mosaic designed by noted Winnipeg artist Leo Mol, the Holy Trinity Ukrainian Orthodox Metropolitan Cathedral is a well-known Main Street landmark. But the museum it hosts at the side of the building is less familiar to many. The Ukrainian Museum of Canada's Manitoba Branch is small, but the intricacy of its exhibits commands your attention. The museum contains collections of Ukrainian folk art and traditional dress, including embroidered ceremonial clothes, multi-coloured woven textiles, and exquisitely decorated eggs.

The colourful outfits you'll find here are adorned with detailed stitchery that may include motifs such as stars, oak leaves, doves, oxen, and other symbols that have been passed down for generations. Note the differences in design and colours from region to region. A long credenza along one wall features clothing and household textiles under glass, with additional display drawers for you to open.

A display of shirt sleeves with Nyzynka embroidery, where the pattern is stitched from the reverse side of the cloth, highlights the intricate details in the embroidery of a single sleeve. Look for the looms, ceramics, and numerous *pysanky*, which are eggs elaborately decorated using a wax-resist method. Don't miss the *lizhnyk*, fluffy wool blankets unique to the Carpathian Mountains. These heavy throws are woven out of pure wool, soaked in a local river or cold water, left to dry, and then combed with a brush.

Take time to read the cards beside the items to learn about the materials used, time period, the region, the creator, and the donor. Most of the artifacts here have been donated, and many were hand-crafted in Ukraine and brought to Manitoba with the first wave of Ukrainian immigrants in the 1890s. Items once part of a family's treasured trunk of belongings are now proudly on display.

Address 1175 Main Street, Winnipeg, MB R2W 3S4, +1 (204) 582-1018, www.umcmb.ca, ukrmuswpg@hotmail.com | Getting there Bus 15 or 18 to Main & Boyd (Stop 30081) or Main & College (Stop 30080) | Hours July & Aug Tue–Sat 10am–4pm and by appointment | Tip Oseredok Ukrainian Cultural and Educational Centre shares Canadian Ukrainian culture through exhibitions, workshops, presentations, and special events (184 Alexander Avenue East, www.oseredok.ca).

106 Upper Fort Garry

Much more than just a wall

The site of Upper Fort Garry Provincial Park in downtown Winnipeg had once been part of Upper Fort Garry, a historic Hudson's Bay Company trading post. The post played a pivotal role in the 1869–1870 Red River Resistance. It was here where an agreement was reached that led to Manitoba becoming Canada's fifth province. An old limestone-and-wood gate at the northern end of the park, which features flower beds and park benches, is all that remains of the original fort, but interpretive plaques and the 400-foot-long Manitoba Liquor & Lotteries Heritage Wall relate the history of the fort and of Manitoba.

The dramatic, modern wall runs along the line of the fort's western boundary and provides a stunning backdrop to the park when viewed from the street. Up close, it is both a work of art and a history lesson. Designs in three layers of Corten Steel, which weathers to a rust colour, represent key elements of Manitoba's history. Viewed from left to right, imagery begins with First Nations, Métis, and the fur trade and continues chronologically. Images include the bison hunt, the Métis sash, voyageurs, maps, animals, the railway, prairie towns, and more. A York Boat and Red River Cart wheel appear in actual size.

A Sound and Light show, using LED lights, video graphics software, and a full-range sound system, recreates the Métis bison hunt every 15 minutes between certain hours. The show starts at the south end and rolls north. Dogs bark as the fort comes to life. The show depicts exiting the fort, encountering a storm, the thunderous bison hunt, the crackling fire to dry the meat, and fiddle music celebrating the end of the hunt.

If your only exposure to the wall has been a glimpse of lights dancing across it while you drive by, come here and visit for a closer look to enjoy the whole experience, as modern technology and artistic design bring history to life.

Address 130 Main Street, Winnipeg, MB, www.upperfortgarry.com, fufg@shaw.ca | Getting there Bus BLUE, 14, 19, 47, or 55 to Main & Assiniboine (Stops 10624/10642) | Hours Unrestricted; see website for sound and light show times | Tip Union Station, built between 1908 and 1911 by the architects of New York's Grand Central Terminal, features a magnificent, high-ceilinged, domed rotunda and Beaux-Arts decorations (123 Main Street).

107 Urban Lumber
A sawmill that recycles Winnipeg's trees

The smell of fresh wood greets you when you enter Urban Lumber's showroom. Most of the furniture Urban Lumber creates are custom pieces, but you'll find a few sample products on display. Run your fingers across smooth slab tables and chairs, plant stands, and cookie slab tables, where the tree rings remain visible. Floating shelves, one of their most popular products, hang on the wall. Laminated hardwood is used to create countertops, mantels, and dining tables. They also sell lumber and live-edge slabs and boards if you want to create your own pieces. In the showroom, look for smaller items, such as bowls or charcuterie boards, crafted by artisans using Urban Lumber's wood.

The wood is salvaged from within Winnipeg and surrounding areas. Urban Lumber can identify which specific neighbourhood the wood in most pieces came from. Arborists supply them with trees removed due to disease, decline, or development. Winnipeg is recognized for having a large concentration of elms, as the city has planted American elms, a native species, on boulevards and in parks since the late 1800s. These trees are susceptible to Dutch elm disease. The City monitors the elms, and each year, diseased trees are sadly marked for removal. Normally, these trees need to be burned or chipped to destroy the fungus, but Urban Lumber has approval from the province and the city to handle diseased wood with strict guidelines. All of their wood is kiln dried, a process that kills the fungus and creates a stable product for furniture.

Urban Lumber's Mike McGarry and Carlee Farmer both grew up in Winnipeg and have forestry backgrounds. They didn't like seeing trees coming down and winding up in the landfill. Their goal is to recycle as many trees as possible and allow people access to the trees. Neighbourhood trees now get second lives as beautiful pieces of furniture in neighbourhood homes.

Address 1289 Loudoun Road, Winnipeg, MB R3S 1A3, +1 (204) 789-8568,
www.urban-lumber.ca, info@urban-lumber.ca | Getting there By car, drive on Wilkes
Avenue to Loudoun Road, turn south | Hours Mon–Fri 9am–5pm, Sat 10am–2pm | Tip
David Perret created the sculpture *We Dream of Flying Canoes* from a diseased, 200-year-old,
landmark elm tree in Whittier Park (836 St. Joseph Street, parkmaps.winnipeg.ca).

108 Waddell Fountain

The price for a widower to remarry

In a downtown park you'll find an elaborate, Gothic-style stone fountain with a steeple-like top – and an unusual story. Central Park, one of eight original "breathing spaces" created by the city's Parks Board, opened in 1894 in what became one of Winnipeg's most exclusive neighbourhoods of the early twentieth century. Waddell Fountain, now designated as a Provincial Heritage Site, was added to the park in 1914. The ornate fountain, which sits atop a granite base, features arches, floral motifs, and pinnacles. Water falls into double-tiered basins from carved lion heads. Each of its four sides is identical.

The fountain is dedicated to Emily Margaret Waddell (1850–1908). Her will stipulated that if her husband Thomas Waddell remarried, he should donate $10,000 to the city for construction of a fountain. The motive behind that request is not known. But Thomas did remarry, and by 1914, he had raised the funds for the fountain. Local architect John Manuel (1879–1933) designed the fountain based on the 1844, Gothic-revival monument to Romantic poet, author, and historian Sir Walter Scott (1771–1832) in Edinburgh, Scotland.

Over the following decades, the upscale homes and grand apartment buildings were subdivided and demolished to make way for high-rises and social housing. The park became rundown and high-risk. And the neglected fountain was in sad shape. After a park revitalization project in 2008–2012 added a pool, spray pad, sand and water play area, and an artificial turf sports area, local families began enjoying the park again. During that time the fountain was also refurbished. It was dismantled into pieces, repaired off-site, reassembled, and placed back in the park.

As you enjoy the beautiful fountain, ponder why Emily Margaret Waddell made that stipulation in her will and imagine what she might think of the structure still standing a century later.

Address 400 Cumberland Avenue, Winnipeg, MB, www.gov.mb.ca/chc/hrb/prov/
p078.html | Getting there Bus 15 to Kennedy & Sargent (Stops 10538/10695) or 11, 14, 15,
19, and more to Portage & Edmonton (Stops 10543/10581) | Hours Daily 7am–10pm | Tip
At the other end of Central Park, the public art piece *DIY Field* features an interactive grid
of 38 light posts that change their lights and colours as visitors interact with them (Central
Park near the corner of Ellice Avenue and Edmonton Street, www.winnipegarts.ca).

109 __ Washroom Box
Award-winning public bathrooms

In Assiniboine Park, adjacent to the outdoor Lyric Theatre and the Tudor-styled Pavilion, three modern, cedar-sided, rectangular structures sit staggered beside each other on a raised wooden deck. A row of trees stands behind them, and a large expanse of lawn spreads out in front. They may remind you of tiny houses in this scenic location. But the letters reading *WASHROOM BOX* on the side of the southernmost structure let you know what they really are: public restrooms. The buildings house three separate restrooms, designated as male, female, and family/accessible.

Looking at the attractive buildings today, you may not immediately realize what they are actually made of. Peter Sampson Architecture Studio and Gardon Construction Ltd. built them from recycled shipping containers obtained from local railways. The containers are insulated on the outside and wrapped in cedar siding on two sides. One end of each 12-metre-long (39-foot-long) container has been removed and replaced with a glass wall and door. Mirrored on the outside and frosted on the inside, the glass reflects the surroundings. Occupants can see out, but people on the outside cannot see in, even at night. The structures were built over a four-month period at a warehouse off site, and the washrooms were trucked to this spot, thereby minimizing disruption to the park during construction.

You'll find the interiors a sharp contrast to the stylish exteriors. Except for the vivid wall colours, different in each washroom, the insides have deliberately been left plain. They are ordinary, unremarkable public restrooms. Back outside, though, you may again be struck by their simple elegance and the way they fit into the surroundings. They no longer appear unremarkable. The Washroom Box won an AZURE Award of Merit for excellence in architecture and a Prairie Design Award of Excellence.

Address 55 Pavilion Crescent, Winnipeg, MB R3P 2N6, +1 (204) 927-6000, www.assiniboine park.ca, info@assiniboinepark.ca | Getting there Bus 18 or 79 to Corydon & Shaftesbury (Stops 60471/60472) or bus 11 or 21 to Portage & Overdale (Stops 20212/20418) | Hours See website for seasonal hours in the park | Tip Recycled shipping containers have also been turned into attractive public restrooms at the popular St. Norbert Farmers' Market (3514 Pembina Highway, www.stnorbertfarmersmarket.ca).

110 Winnipeg Police Museum

North America's first three-digit emergency number

The Winnipeg Police Museum, located at Winnipeg Police headquarters, displays artifacts about the city's history of policing from the 1894 creation of the Winnipeg Police Force to the present day. Among the many exhibits, you'll find a number of innovations and firsts, such as North America's first three-digit emergency telephone system.

The emergency system switchboard would be considered quaint and old-fashioned now, but it was leading edge when it was implemented in 1959. At the time, separate police and fire departments had their own phone numbers. With the implementation of the emergency number system, people needed only to dial 999 to reach an operator, who then dispatched the call through to the appropriate department by plugging the phone cable into its associated socket.

Eight emergency operators, all women, staffed the centre in the beginning. Helen Woolard (1929–2013) was their first supervisor. The decision to employ women was a budgetary one, as the city paid women $250 a month vs. $345 for men.

Dialing 999 on the older rotary phones in the display required a complete rotation of the dial three times in a row. So, the 999 emergency number was changed to the simpler and faster 911 in 1972. The call board was retired in 1990 due to new and improved technology.

Also look for handcuffs, firearms, mug shot cameras, fingerprint cards, and speed enforcement tools. There are uniforms, police log books, "Wanted" posters, vehicles, a jail cell, and stories of Winnipeg's most notorious criminals. You'll get a glimpse into the broader city history and the social climate in which the police have operated. Don't miss the call boxes introduced in 1913 and the K9 Storm, the world's first custom-fitted body armour for police dogs, created by Constable Jim Slater in 1998.

Address 245 Smith Street, Winnipeg, MB R3C 0R6, +1 (204) 986-3976, www.winnipegpolicemuseum.ca, wps-museum@winnipeg.ca | Getting there Bus BLUE, 16, 17, 18, 20, 33, 44, 45, or 60 to Graham & Garry (Stop 10612), Garry & Graham (Stop 10650), or Graham & Smith (Stop 10615) or bus 10, 11, 14, 15, 19, 21, 24, 38, 43, or 55 to Portage & Donald (Stops 10542/10582) | Hours Tue–Fri 10am–3pm; see website for extended hours in July & Aug | Tip See the restored Rupert Avenue Station Monument and old fire and police call boxes along St Mary Avenue at Smith Street just outside the museum.

111 — The Witch's Hut

A "Hansel and Gretel" house in Kildonan Park

Nestled amid century-old elm trees beside a creek and surrounded by ferns and flowers, the round, stone building with a pointed roof of wooden shakes looks like something straight out of a fairy tale book. Although its shape differs from that of the traditional gingerbread house, the Witch's Hut brings to life the Grimm Brothers' "Hansel and Gretel". Designed by well-known Manitoba architect Peter Langes with masonry and handcrafted woodwork completed by John Nelson, the Witch's Hut was a 1970 Centennial project of the German Community of Manitoba and a gift to the children of the province.

Step through the red door into a fairy tale world. A stone wall circles around a central round stone chimney. Heavy wood chairs and a table sit along the wall. Wood beams slant towards the peak of the roof. A partial second level creates a low wood-beamed ceiling in half of the space. Relief terracotta panels, created by sculptress Elfriede Berger, run around the circumference at eye level and recreate the "Hansel and Gretel" story in sequential scenes. In the fairy tale, two children, held captive by a witch in a gingerbread hut after they get lost in the woods, escape before she eats them. Notice how the expressions on the faces in the panels add to the story. Look for animals and birds tucked into the forest. Climb the circular wooden staircase to a "Hansel and Gretel" scene, complete with wood-burning stove, quilt-covered bed, a table and shelves holding household and decorative items, and full-scale images of Hansel, Gretel, and the witch, all handcrafted by Josef Potempa.

The interior of the hut is open to the public during select times in summer months, but the exterior is viewable any time of year during Kildonan Park's open hours. Sit for a while on the bench alongside the pathway in front of the hut, admire the idyllic setting – and keep an eye out for the witch.

Address 2015 Main Street, Winnipeg, MB R2V 2B9, legacy.winnipeg.ca/publicworks/
parksOpenSpace/ParkRentals/BookableParks/WitchsHut.stm | **Getting there** Bus 18
and 77 to Main & Kildonan Park (Stops 30023/30024) | **Hours** Exterior daily 7am–10pm;
see website for interior seasonal hours | **Tip** Walking paths meander through colourful
flowers and shrubs in Kildonan Park's North Garden while benches offer a chance to just sit
and enjoy the beauty (2015 Main Street, parkmaps.winnipeg.ca).

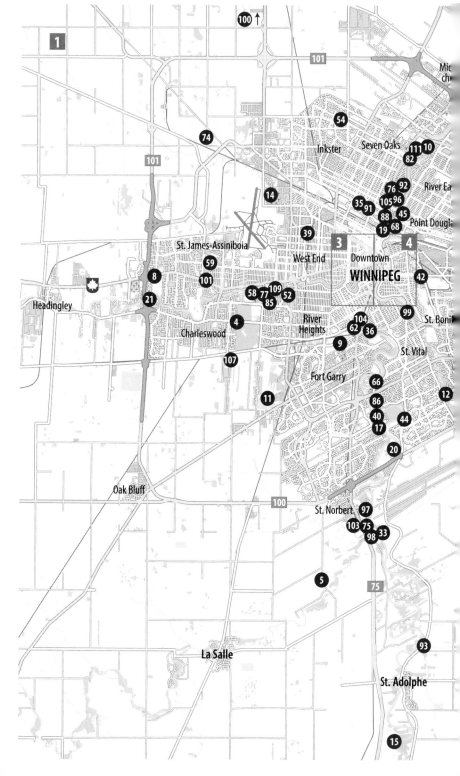

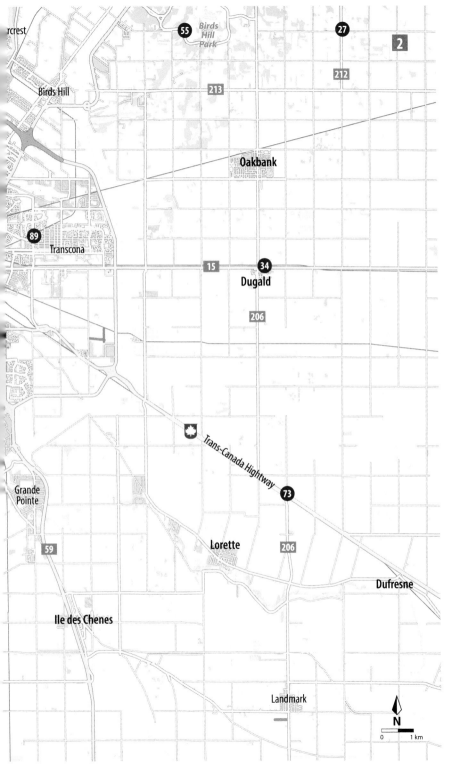

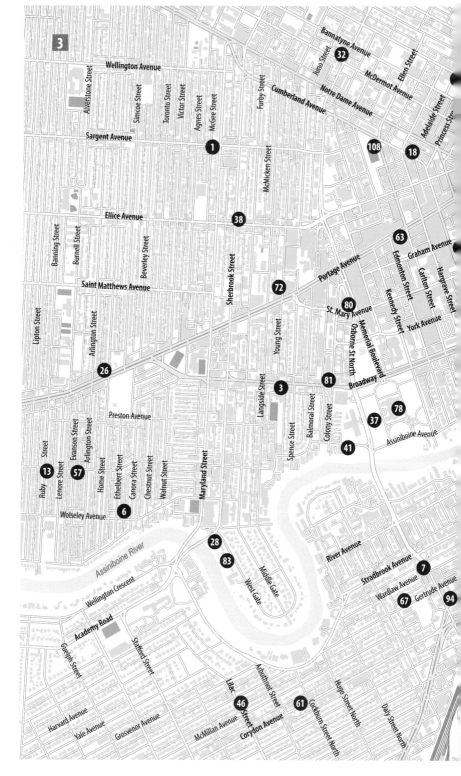

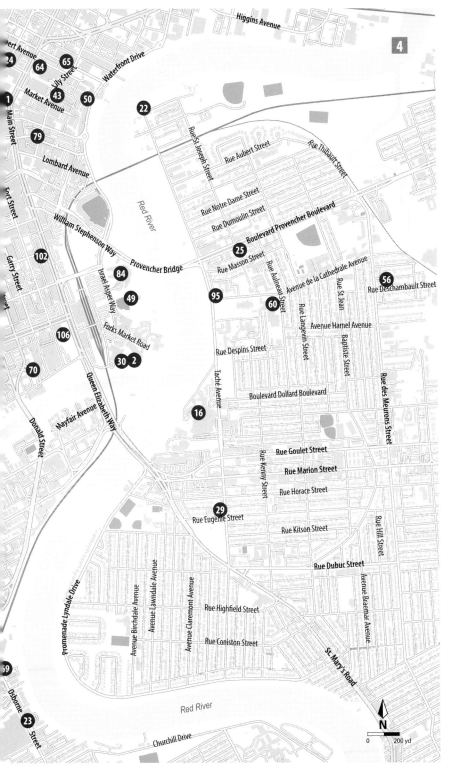

Kaitlyn McInnis,
Bethany Livingstone
111 Places in Montreal
That You Must Not Miss
ISBN 978-3-7408-1721-3

Dave Doroghy, Graeme Menzies
111 Places in Victoria
That You Must Not Miss
ISBN 978-3-7408-1720-6

Dave Doroghy, Graeme Menzies
111 Places in Vancouver
That You Must Not Miss
ISBN 978-3-7408-2150-0

Dave Doroghy, Graeme Menzies
111 Places in Whistler
That You Must Not Miss
ISBN 978-3-7408-1046-7

Jennifer Bain, Liz Beddall
111 Places in Ottawa
That You Must Not Miss
ISBN 978-3-7408-1388-8

Jennifer Bain, Christina Ryan
111 Places in Calgary
That You Must Not Miss
ISBN 978-3-7408-1559-2

Elizabeth Lenell-Davies,
Anita Genua, Claire Davenport
111 Places in Toronto
That You Must Not Miss
ISBN 978-3-7408-0257-8

Jo-Anne Elikann, Susan Lusk
111 Places in New York
That You Must Not Miss
ISBN 978-3-7408-2400-6

Wendy Lubovich, Ed Lefkowicz
111 Museums in New York
That You Must Not Miss
ISBN 978-3-7408-2374-0

Brian Hayden, Jesse Pitzler
**111 Places in Buffalo
That You Must Not Miss**
ISBN 978-3-7408-2151-7

Kim Windyka, Heather Kapplow,
Alyssa Wood
**111 Places in Boston
That You Must Not Miss**
ISBN 978-3-7408-2056-5

Andréa Seiger, John Dean
**111 Places in Washington
That You Must Not Miss**
ISBN 978-3-7408-2399-3

Brandon Schultz, Lucy Baber
**111 Places in Philadelphia
That You Must Not Miss**
ISBN 978-3-7408-1376-5

Amy Bizzarri, Susie Inverso
**111 Places in Chicago
That You Must Not Miss**
ISBN 978-3-7408-1030-6

Michelle Madden, Janet McMillan
**111 Places in Milwaukee
That You Must Not Miss**
ISBN 978-3-7408-1643-8

Harriet Baskas, Curtney Kelley
**111 Places in Seattle
That You Must Not Miss**
ISBN 978-3-7408-2375-7

Floriana Petersen, Steve Werney
**111 Places in San Francisco
That You Must Not Miss**
ISBN 978-3-7408-2058-9

Laurel Moglen, Julia Posey,
Lyudmila Zotova
**111 Places in Los Angeles
That You Must Not Miss**
ISBN 978-3-7408-1889-0

Photo Credits

Bison Safari (ch. 11): FortWhyte Alive, Mike Peters

Crokicurl at The Forks (ch. 30): The Forks, Kristhine Guerrero

Manitoba Museum (ch. 64): original John A. Robinson photograph from Manitoba Archives

Riel House (ch. 86): Shauna Turnley / ©Parks Canada / Riel House National Historic Site

The REDress Project (ch. 84): Courtesy of The Canadian Museum for Human Rights, photograph by Ian McCausland

Art Credits

A Man Called Intrepid (ch. 1): by Dave Carty

Back Alley Arctic (ch. 6): *Back Alley Arctic* by Kal Barteski

Beaumont Station (ch. 9): *Rooster Town Kettle* by Ian August

Bois-des-Esprits (ch. 12): Carvings by Murray Watson

Bonnie Day (ch. 13): *Untitled* (*Winnipeg Map*) © Marcel Dzama, courtesy the artist and David Zwirner

Cornish Library (ch. 28): *Our Cornish Library and the Suffrage Saga* by Naomi Gerrard

Famous Five Monument (ch. 37): *Famous Five Monument* by Helen Granger Young

Jai Pereira Memorial (ch. 49): *Jai Pereira Mural* by Mr Cenz

Louis Riel Statue (ch. 60): *Louis Riel Statue* by Marcien Lemay and Étienne Gaboury

MICEC (ch. 68): Carving by Rick Hall

Porter-Milady Ghost Sign (ch. 79): *Porter-Milady Installation* by Craig Winslow and Matt Cohen

The REDress Project (ch. 84): *The REDress Project* by Jaime Black

Residential School Totem Pole (ch. 85): *The Story of the Residential School Totem Pole* by Charles Joseph

St. Boniface Heritage Garden (ch. 95): *Spiritu Vocat Appel de l'esprit Spirit's Call* by Madeleine Vrignon

I want to thank my husband Rick Melia for his patience, encourage-ment, and advice during the writing of the book and always. Thanks to all my family and friends for their support. A special shout-out to Terry Wiebe, who has joined me in many city explorations over the years. To my writing group friends Joan, Kim, and Nancy, I appre-ciate your encouragement and interest in this project even as it took me away from the fiction writing that is my focus with the group. I am grateful to all Winnipeg writers and historians whose articles and podcasts continue to lead me to discover more about my home city. A great big thank you to those who talked with me about your work and passions. I am honoured to share your stories. To Gin Ouskun, thanks for the lovely photographs. I enjoyed visiting places together and get-ting to know you. Thanks to everyone at Emons Verlag and especially to Karen Seiger for guiding me through the process, encouraging me, and bringing out the best in my writing.

Donna Janke

Thank you so much to my husband Drew Drabik for supporting and encouraging me throughout the project. I couldn't have done it without you. An extra- special thank you to my son Bennett, who visited almost every location with me. It was the most exciting and challenging mater-nity leave – I wouldn't change a thing. To my family and friends, who supported me and even joined me on car rides when I went to photo-graph the city. I'm so grateful to have made connections with everyone I met along the way. You really made learning about my home even more special. It was truly an unforgettable experience. I'm so lucky to have met and worked with you, Donna Janke. Thank you for the conversa-tions and for letting me visit places with you. Thank you to everyone at Emons Verlag, especially Karen Seiger, for taking a chance on me.

Gindalee Ouskun

Donna Janke is a travel writer from the Canadian prairies. She loves to explore wherever she finds herself, discover the many facets of each place, and share those stories through her writing. She applies that same curiosity to her home city of Winnipeg and delights in showcasing its unique character.

Gindalee Ouskun is a Treaty One Territory/ Winnipeg-based photographer and has appreciated rediscovering the city while taking the photos for this book. Gindalee specializes in lifestyle and wedding photography, and she works closely with the Manitoban Indigenous community. In her downtime, she enjoys spending time with her husband and son, and travelling and hiking with her mini Aussie. www.ginouskunphoto.com

The information in this book was accurate at the time of publication, but it can change at any time. Please confirm the details for the places you're planning to visit before you head out on your adventures.